THEY SAW THE JAGUAR ROUND THE CORNER.

❏

Rick Ames slowed to turn right on Quebec. They could see him lighting a cigarette.

Guerin had been leery of this part of the operation. Suppose Rick panicked, thinking it was a holdup, and tried to run up the sidewalk and across the lawn? Suppose somebody chose that moment to come out of the front door? Suppose Rick had a gun nobody knew about?

But Rick would have no time to think about anything.

Mike Donner started flashing a red light that sat on his dashboard. He turned on his siren. Rick slowed toward the curb, as if to let Donner pass him. He stopped a few feet short of one of the SWAT cars. Donner came up to the rear of the Jaguar.

He sprang from his car. Dell Spry came around from the other side, gun in hand. Rick, looking bewildered behind his thick glasses, was rolling down his window. A Benson & Hedges cigarette dangled between his lips. Donner reached in and jerked it away. "FBI," Donner said, holding up his badge, "You're under arrest!" Then Donner opened the door and yanked Rick into the street.

"For what?" Rick cried. "For what?"

"For espionage," Donner said. "Put your hands on the roof of your car."

"What!" Rick cried again. "This is unbeliev-able. *Unbelievable!"*

❏

PETER MAAS

KILLER SPY

WARNER BOOKS

A Time Warner Company

WARNER BOOKS EDITION

Copyright © 1995 by J. M. M. Productions, Inc.
All rights reserved.

Cover design by Bernadette Evangelist
Cover photograph by Stephen Jaffe/J.B. Pictures

Warner Books, Inc.
1271 Avenue of the Americas
New York, NY 10020

W A Time Warner Company

ISBN: 0-446-60279-5
ISBN: 978-0-446-60279-2

Printed in the United States of America

Originally published in hardcover by Warner Books.
First Printed in Paperback: February, 1996

10 9 8 7 6 5 4 3 2 1

This is for Wayne Kabak

AUTHOR'S NOTE

It will be readily apparent to the reader that this book could not have been written without exceptional cooperation from the Federal Bureau of Investigation.

This is because, on the record, I was the first author to request such cooperation, while others initially devoted themselves to trying to gain access to Aldrich H. Ames. I myself once met with Ames to ascertain what he was like. It became immediately clear to me that he was the last person who would be able to cast true light on who he was, much less what he had done, during his nine-year run as the most treacherous spy in American history.

It seemed equally clear to me that the real story of Ames was how he was pursued and captured by the FBI, which is what is presented on the pages that follow. A corollary to this, of course, is how he managed to escape the notice of his superiors in the Central Intelligence Agency for so long.

Despite the cooperation of the FBI, there were sensitive issues that it resisted revealing. So I also turned to the CIA itself and to other sources with an intimate knowledge of the case and its participants.

Peter Maas
March 8, 1995

KILLER
SPY

PROLOGUE

By early 1981, with the cold war raging nonstop, FBI counterintelligence (CI) had embarked on a new approach toward suspected Soviet intelligence officers active in the United States. Instead of keeping them under passive surveillance or waiting for volunteers who "walk in" as sources, an aggressive, selective effort would be made to recruit them on behalf of American interests.

As part of this new approach, an experimental undercover team with the code name Courtship was handpicked from members of the twenty-two counterintelligence squads then attached to the FBI's Washington Field Office. Also novel was the inclusion in Courtship of CIA officers. It was the first time that the FBI and the CIA, with their antagonistic history, had combined operational forces.

Almost at once, Valery Martynov, a major in the KGB, the Soviet intelligence service, became a prime Courtship target.

Thirty-six years old, dark-haired, about six feet tall, and somewhat overweight, he had arrived in

Washington on November 4, 1980—the day Ronald Reagan was first elected president—accompanied by his wife, Natalya, to whom he was devoted, and two small children, a boy and a girl. It was his first overseas duty tour. Ostensibly, he was third secretary for cultural affairs in the embassy, handling academic and student exchanges. In fact, he specialized in gathering scientific and technological intelligence and had been invited to join the KGB in 1970 right after graduating with honors in computer science from a prestigious Moscow technical institute.

Surveillance reports also indicated that Martynov had all the qualities Courtship was on the lookout for: He was a stable, family-oriented man who drank sparingly, an energetic officer who faithfully followed all the do's and don't's of the intelligence game. But more important, they showed that he despised what the corrupt Soviet system was doing to Mother Russia. "He's not a happy camper," one report said. "He feels shat upon." He was overheard to complain bitterly, "It's not what you do, but who you know that matters." A psychological profile of Martynov posited that he had joined the KGB "not as a calling, but a job, a way to gain entry into the Soviet ruling elite, to insure his family's future well-being."

An FBI undercover agent in Courtship named Bill Mann, equipped with an alias and false identity papers, began to frequent the scientific and technical seminars and trade shows that Valery Martynov attended. Mann made it a point to remain noticeably aloof from the rest of the crowd, as if an observer of the goings-on. Other Courtship undercover agents were also present. One of them struck up an acquaintanceship with Martynov, who eventually inquired about Mann and was told that he was a consultant in the scientific community with big-time relationships in both the government and private enterprise.

Then the crucial first step in the seduction occurred. Martynov made the initial overture to Mann. While not admitting, of course, that he was a KGB officer, he confessed that he wanted technology to help a Soviet Union backward in so many areas, and Mann allowed as that in his opinion a free exchange of information would probably make for a better and safer world. The two men started socializing. Mann steered Martynov to Courtship agents who supplied hard-to-get, although unclassified, manuals and documents. When Martynov sought out other American contacts, they were immediately investigated for their access to classified material and any personal vulnerabilities they might have. If they passed muster, their cooperation was requested, and, without exception, was forthcoming.

Now, convinced that he was building and in control of a burgeoning intelligence network, Martynov himself was being controlled. Agent Mann could turn the spigot on and off at will. He gave Martynov good weeks and bad ones. During the bad ones, the KGB major, worried about his career, got increasingly panicky.

Once, at a computer software convention, he followed Mann into a men's room and at the urinal pressed him for details on a new Lotus program.

Mann purposely exploded, "For Christ's sake, Valery, lay off, will you? Can't you see I'm taking a leak?"

Aghast at the prospect of falling out of Mann's good graces, Martynov apologized profusely, which only enhanced his dependency on the Courtship agent.

After a couple of months, however, Martynov began pushing for more sensitive data. Without getting into specifics, Mann said that he had "a friend" in the intelligence community who possibly could supply it, but the friend would want something in return. "Listen, Valery," Mann explained, "this is D.C. This is how the game is played. You know, tit for tat."

What did Mann think his friend had in mind?

Oh, maybe the identities of some intelligence officers at the embassy, or perhaps some target areas.

A week later, Martynov nervously passed on two names. Mann handed him cash in return, an appreciative gift from his friend. The amount was a modest five hundred dollars. But when Martynov took it, a threshold with no return had been crossed. And they both knew it.

There were two more exchanges of cash before it was time to turn Martynov over to a handler. Mann eased into it. At first he said, "Hey, look, Valery, I don't really know about this stuff we're getting into. I need an expert to take over." Then he announced, "I'm leaving town. I've got a big new job in California, but trust me, you'll be in good hands."

FBI agent Jim Holt, Martynov's handler, was in squad CI-5, which tracked known KGB scientific and technological intelligence collectors. Martynov was forever jumpy about his own security, always worried about what might go wrong. Even with Mann, he never allowed his voice to be recorded, and if he made a request in writing, he made Mann rewrite it and destroyed the original. So Holt had been especially chosen to deal with him. A veteran counterintelligence agent, he had an engaging, quietly confident demeanor. You automatically felt that in his presence there was nothing to be concerned about.

Holt and Martynov first met one April night in 1982 in a northern Virginia parking lot. More than a year had gone by since Bill Mann began his painstaking recruitment. Since the case had started under Courtship auspices, a CIA officer also was on hand, although Holt took the lead. Martynov never knew that Mann was FBI, but from that moment on, while FBI,

CIA, or KGB was never actually mentioned, everyone involved knew who was who and what was at stake.

From the parking lot, they adjourned to one of the three safe houses that would be used for meetings. The meetings took place every two weeks, either at lunchtime or in the evening when Martynov's absence from work would not draw undue attention. Platters of sandwiches were supplied, and if an evening meeting had been scheduled, a beer or two would be consumed before conducting business.

In driving to a safe house, Martynov took great care to "dry clean" himself, expertly wheeling in and out of cul-de-sacs, for example, to make sure he wasn't being followed. Additionally, he was always covered by FBI surveillance teams. After each meeting, he would receive three hundred dollars in cash. Holt soon stopped warning him not to do anything flashy with the money. Martynov was cautious to a fault. The only purchases out of the ordinary he ever made were a computer for his twelve-year-old son and a birthday mink coat for his wife. Even the mink, should embassy eyebrows be raised, was bought on an installment plan.

Fifteen hundred dollars a month also was set aside for him in an escrow account. The money satisfied part of Martynov's concern about future security for his family. The other part was success in his KGB career. He never evidenced any interest in defecting. Holt suggested, and Martynov agreed, that he would be supplied with one solid source at any given time, with three others in development—just enough to keep his superiors happy, but not excite their curiosity.

Over time, Holt grew rather fond of Martynov. To alleviate the pressure that always hovered over them, he encouraged small talk. They both had daughters about the same age and often reflected on the pleasures and pitfalls of parenthood. When Martynov's son developed a severe respiratory ailment, Holt steered him to a lung specialist who treated the problem. Martynov started essaying small jokes. "Ah," he said, "your emissary from the Evil Empire has arrived." Another time, he expressed real regret at the 1983 downing of the Korean jetliner by the Soviets that cost so many American lives. Under other circumstances, Holt would often think, they could have been true friends.

Valery Martynov revealed the identities of more than fifty Soviet intelligence officers operating out of the embassy, a number of whom the FBI was unaware of. And the information saved counterintelligence agents the trouble of chasing suspects who, in fact, were not spies. He also disclosed scores of technical and scientific targets that the KGB was after, or had penetrated, enabling the FBI to plug the leaks or pass back disinformation.

The only thing Martynov could not give up were the names of any Americans, if, indeed, there were any, in the FBI, CIA, or other national security agencies who were working on behalf of the Soviets. The KGB's internal security compartmentalization was just too good.

Aside from that, as the FBI's John Lewis, who headed up Courtship, could exult, Martynov "was a gold mine."

Around the time Martynov became "operational," quite apart from Courtship, a second KGB intelligence officer at the Soviet embassy, Sergei Motorin, was finally recruited by the FBI. The KGB was divided into branches that it called "lines." Motorin was in Line PR, which pursued political and policy intelligence. His cover was Washington correspondent for the semiofficial press agency Novosti.

Like Martynov, Motorin held the rank of major,

spoke excellent English, was married with two young children, and was on his first duty tour outside the USSR. All similarities ended right there.

Thirty years old, Motorin was strikingly handsome, six feet four inches tall, with a dazzling smile, an athletic build that he took great pride in, carefully coiffed swept back blond hair, and a neatly trimmed pencil mustache.

He had graduated at the top of his class from Moscow's Institute for International Relations with a degree in journalism. A year later, he was taken into the KGB, helped no little by the connections of his new wife, Olga, whose father was an officer in the GRU, the military intelligence arm of the Soviet General Staff, and whose mother had worked for the NKVD, Stalin's dreaded secret police.

But Sergei Motorin was not a man made for the monogamous life. Within a few months after his arrival, in mid-1980, he began to cut a wide swath through women at the Soviet compound, both married and single, who were overwhelmed by his rakish charm. He was regularly out on the town at the better restaurants and bars, where he downed vodka with abandon. And he quickly got the attention of squad CI-2, which targeted suspected Line PR intelligence officers, by the blatant way he probed for inside U.S. political and foreign policy intentions on Capitol Hill, at the State Department, and among media people.

Then CI-2 figured it had a real hook into Motorin when surveillance caught him in an electronics store slipping bottles of vodka from the embassy commissary to a sales clerk in return for stereo equipment.

Agent Mike Morton went to the store management, explained that this was a case involving national security, and concluded a deal whereby the sales clerk would not be punished if he continued to service

Motorin. The FBI would reimburse the store for any equipment it lost.

The next time Motorin dropped by the store for another vodka transaction, Morton, operating undercover, was on hand. The clerk introduced him as "a government official" and, with a wink at the Russian, added that Morton was another of his customers, "just like you."

Motorin wasn't fazed a bit. Smiling broadly, he said to Morton, "Well, we have a lot in common. You work for your government and I work for mine. And we're both crooks. Let's go have a drink."

Clearly, holding Motorin's black market activities over his head wasn't going to provide the hoped-for leverage. But at least a connection had been made, and agent Morton began bouncing around Washington with Motorin, substituting water for his vodka whenever he could. Any pretense of the delicate dance a recruitment usually entailed vanished one night when Motorin said, "Look, I like you. I'm probably KGB and you're probably FBI. Why don't we just have a good time together and forget the rest."

Now Mike Morton hammered relentlessly at Motorin, pitching him repeatedly. "Sergei," he'd say, "we know all about you. You're screwing every woman you can get your hands on. You're headed for a tumble. What about your wife? She could cause you a lot of pain the way you're carrying on. Get you sent back to Moscow on your first tour. That won't look so good on the old résumé. We can help you, help your career. You give us some stuff, we'll do the same. Get you promoted."

Motorin waved him off. "I'm the best thing that ever happened to Olga," he said. "You know what most Russian men are like in bed?" He hesitated and, with just a hint of uncertainty, added, "I'm good at my job. It's those bureaucratic assholes who don't appreciate it." Finally, though, he looked straight at Morton and said, "I'm not in the business of betraying my country."

Morton had a sneaking admiration for Motorin's high-wire act, as self-destructive as it was, but he wouldn't give up. "Just wait," he said. "You'll see I'm right."

The magic moment came after Motorin returned from home leave. Motorin couldn't imagine how miserable conditions in the Soviet Union had become, he said. Life in Washington had allowed him to overlook how corrupt the ruling elite was, how incredibly downtrodden ordinary citizens were, the despair that buffeted their daily existence. Then he said, in a tone etched in resignation, "You know, I think I'd be doing my people a favor working with the FBI against the KGB."

They began meeting in safe houses, only the two of them. Motorin refused to be turned over to a handler. It would be Mike Morton or nobody. And no CIA. It was as if he had created an imaginary world in which two pals were simply trading favors, helping one another out, a world where there was no Soviet Union, no United States.

His information didn't compare with Martynov's, nor was he paid as much—"With my expenses, I can use the money," he said—but Morton believed that Motorin was still holding back, that there was much more to come.

Suddenly, it ended. Their last meeting was on January 3, 1985. Two days later, without warning, Motorin was on a plane to Moscow.

At first, it was feared that he had been blown. But Martynov, who had identified him as KGB, reported that Sergei Motorin had gone too far in his philandering. He had been found bedded down with the secretary of a high-ranking embassy official. Internal security officers decided he had become too much of a risk. Who knew? His next bed companion might be an American agent.

His identity and code name "Meges" (from one of the Greek warriors hidden in the Trojan horse) were turned over to the CIA for its possible utilization of him behind the Iron Curtain or wherever else he might be reassigned.

For him, as well as for Martynov, winding up in CIA files would prove to have lethal consequences.

Martynov, meanwhile, continued to provide information to Jim Holt and his CIA counterpart. Then, during the summer of 1985, the intelligence community was rocked by the defection of the most important KGB officer the CIA had ever had fall into its hands— Colonel Vitaly Yurchenko, who was about to assume command of all KGB intelligence operations in the United States and Canada. In his debriefings by the CIA and FBI, he delivered a wealth of information that led among other things to the unmasking of a former CIA officer, Edward Lee Howard, and a former National Security Agency employee, Ronald Pelton, as Soviet agents. But even after Yurchenko was assured of at least a million dollars and protection in the United States, he insisted that he could not point to a currently active mole the Soviets might have in the CIA.

Yurchenko had demanded that his defection be kept secret. However, then CIA director William Casey couldn't resist crowing about it all over Washington, and he became headline news.

In late October, as this was going on, Holt had a safe house meeting with Martynov and noticed that the Soviet was limping noticeably. He'd suffered a bad fall, he said, and damaged the meniscus cartilage in his knee. He was hoping prescribed exercises would do the trick to avoid surgery. His doctor, he said, had advised that losing some weight would certainly help.

Then, on the evening of November 2, a Saturday, the CIA's great prize, Yurchenko, after finishing off a meal featuring poached salmon with his security guard at a restaurant in Washington's Georgetown neighborhood, walked out and never came back. The CIA was frantic.

Valery Martynov had been given a pager number by Holt to call in the event of an emergency. The call was to be made from a preassigned phone booth. Another booth would get the return call. Twenty-four hours after Yurchenko strolled off into the night, the pager was activated.

"Yurchenko, we have him," Martynov told Holt. He said there would be a press conference the next afternoon, Monday, at the new embassy compound in the Mount Alto section of Washington.

At the press conference, Yurchenko announced that he was not a defector at all, that he had been seized by CIA operatives in Rome, Italy, drugged, and flown to the United States, where he was held captive until he managed to escape.

Later that evening, using the pager again, Martynov reported that he was going to be part of the team escorting Yurchenko back to Moscow. They'd be leaving on Wednesday from Dulles Airport. "I should be back in a week or so," he said.

On television, Holt watched Yurchenko's departure. He saw Martynov. It was the last time he saw him.

But there was no immediate cause for concern when he did not show up again as promised. Ten days later, Martynov's wife received word that her husband's knee condition was worse than had been thought and required extensive surgery. A few days afterward another communication from Moscow came. Martynov wanted her and their children to be with him.

So far, everything appeared normal. For about five months, his apartment in Alexandria, Virginia, remained untouched, furniture in place, as if in expectation of his imminent return. All at once, however, in early April 1986, the apartment was closed down, the furniture removed.

Still, the Iron Curtain was the Iron Curtain, and there was a lot of mystery behind it. Rumors, for instance, circulated that Yurchenko had been summarily executed. Then it turned out that he was alive and well in Moscow and working on security measures for Soviet diplomats abroad. Had he been a true defector or was something else involved here?

In the midst of all this, the CIA began relaying tidbits that Martynov—*and* Motorin—were in deep trouble, possibly in prison, even dead. Angry and frustrated at their probable loss, the FBI commenced a study lasting many months in an attempt to discover what had gone wrong. *Had* something gone wrong?

Perhaps not. A call was intercepted from Motorin in Moscow to the girlfriend he'd been caught in bed with that had caused his hasty exit from Washington. Don't worry, he told her. He'd been on special assignments he couldn't discuss. He missed her and hoped to see her soon. Agent Mike Morton attested that it was Motorin's voice, apparently as jaunty as ever.

This turned out to be a KGB ruse. By the summer of 1987, definitive word came that both men were indeed dead. Later, it would turn out that Martynov, ever the fatalist, had matter-of-factly recounted his FBI recruitment and faced a firing squad. But Motorin's KGB inquisitors, enraged by his defiantly insouciant ways, saw to it that he suffered a hideously tortured end.

And nearly nine years would pass from that day Jim Holt watched Martynov board a plane at Dulles before the FBI learned that far more than a mole was in place deep within the CIA.

He was a cold-blooded serial killer.

1

At Buzzard Point in the drug-ravaged, murder-prone Anacostia ghetto of the nation's capital, the ugly box-like structure that housed the FBI's Washington Field Office fit right in with the immediate neighborhood. Across the way, on potholed Half Street, was a grimy substation of the Potomac Electric Power Company. The vacant, refuse-strewn fields nearby featured a scrap metal yard and a repository for piles of used tires, which periodically caught fire. Two blocks distant was a garishly painted nightclub where fatal early morning shootouts regularly occurred. The absurdity of it all actually gave agents assigned to the Washington Field Office a unique raffish élan in the FBI.

From his corner eleventh-floor office, the special agent in charge, Robert Bryant, could look down at the garbage eddying in the Anacostia River as it flowed into the Potomac a quarter mile downstream. Every so often, Bryant would spot a Potomac-bound corpse and buzz his secretary, "Call the cops. There's another floater in the river."

Bryant's nickname was "the Bear." It wasn't because of the famous Alabama football coach. When he was a ten-year-old kid, a schoolyard bully started picking on him, and before long, the bully was running home in tears, screaming, "That Bobby Bryant bit me like a bear!" And the truth was that at five feet ten, with his amiable face, ample girth, and shambling gait, he resembled a friendly ursine. But the sobriquet stuck because everyone who ever worked with him knew that when Bryant sank his teeth in a case, he hung on ferociously until it was resolved one way or the other.

Born in Springfield, Missouri, in 1943, with a law degree from the University of Arkansas, Bryant had spent most of his FBI career combating organized crime and had risen fast in its ranks. In the late 1970s, he was running the FBI's Las Vegas Field Office when the Mafia and corrupt Teamsters officials still had a stranglehold over the city's casinos. Later, in Kansas City, he took on Cosa Nostra's Civello crime family, one of the most violent in the country's underworld.

He assumed command of the Washington Field Office in July 1991. At the time, the focus there, utilizing well over half its personnel, was on foreign counterintelligence. But the way bear Bryant saw things, an investigation was an investigation. Whether it was the Mob or the KGB, you tried to develop assets or informants for either prosecution or information. Of course, there were nuances in technique, and on that score he could always rely on the counsel of his chief assistant, John Lewis, who had headed up the Courtship program and was unmatched in his knowledge and experience in both covert and overt counterintelligence.

About a year after Bryant set up shop at Buzzard Point, a young counterintelligence agent named Les Wiser Jr. approached him about making a career change. Wiser had been in CI-7, the East German squad. After the Berlin Wall came down in 1989, the squad transferred its attention to overseas espionage, looking into allegations of spying in U.S. embassies and consulates. Wiser had especially loved the cat-and-mouse play with the highly professional East German intelligence service. Thwarting it had meant something, but suddenly the challenge was gone. He became increasingly demoralized with all the media reports and pronouncements from Capitol Hill that the cold war was over. Besides, the word around the field office was that Bear Bryant intended to devote much more of the office's resources to fighting gang violence and drug trafficking in the District of Columbia. Maybe, he thought, both for his own psychic well-being and for his FBI future, he ought to switch to purely criminal casework.

To his surprise, however, Bryant said, "Why don't you stick with CI for a while, at least another six months or so."

However casually delivered, a suggestion like that from the Bear was tantamount to a directive. So Wiser stayed put. He was rewarded with his own CI squad, one that was supposed to target countries largely ignored during the cold war—Asian countries like Pakistan and Japan, other nations in the Middle East, still more on the African continent, all intent on harvesting key U.S. political, economic, and technological intelligence. Wiser started with only five agents, who had been more or less working on their own, not even enough to warrant an official supervisor. But in short order, he developed a strategic plan and built a highly motivated squad that had other CI agents eager to join, none of which escaped Bryant's notice.

What Wiser hadn't known when he spoke to Bryant about a career path change was that just prior to the Bear's arrival at Buzzard Point the biggest spy case in U.S. history had begun to percolate—one that would subsequently occupy Wiser's every waking moment and intrude night after night in his sleep.

In the spring of 1991, Paul Redmond, the deputy chief of the CIA's Counterintelligence Center, had requested a meeting at FBI headquarters with Ray Mislock, section chief for the former Soviet Union in the bureau's Division 5, which was responsible for protecting the country's national security.

It was not a pleasant visit for Redmond. He had a shocking admission. "We have blood on our hands," he confessed to Mislock. "We think there's been a major penetration within the agency."

And for the first time, the FBI became privy to the full extent of what had been going on, confirming its worst fears. Since the executions of Valery Martynov and Sergei Motorin, the FBI now learned that another of its informants, dating back thirty years to 1961, had been executed as well, a man who was a general in GRU military intelligence and who—after he was turned over to the CIA upon departing the United States—became perhaps the CIA's finest source for a staggering range of Soviet secrets. And there was still a fourth casualty, a KGB lieutenant colonel developed by the San Francisco Field Office, who, following his return to the Soviet Union and his cooperation made known to the CIA for its potential use, had simply vanished—to a fate yet to be determined.

There was more. A shamefaced CIA itself had lost at least a half dozen Soviet sources recruited overseas to firing squads or worse—a KGB training film showed a shackled betrayer being lowered slowly into a blast furnace. And another score or more had been sentenced to Gulag slave labor camps.

The situation was so desperate that the unthinkable was about to take place. With the authorization of then CIA director (and former FBI director) Judge

William Webster, the CIA was without qualification
inviting in the FBI's investigative know-how. Not
since its formation in 1947 had the agency allowed
access not simply to summaries, but to raw files, every
available detail about every case that showed signs of
having suffered a deadly compromise.

The FBI code name for the probe was Playactor.

It was divided into two parts. In the first, two
agents from headquarters, Jim Holt and Jim Milburn,
would work with two senior female CIA analysts at
the agency's Langley, Virginia, nerve center to try to
pinpoint where and how human penetration of the
agency had occurred—who the Soviet mole might be,
for there was no longer any doubt that there was one.

Holt and Milburn were judicious choices. There
still remained a wide cultural gap between the bureau
and the agency. Many elements in the CIA continued
to look down their noses at the FBI as a bunch of
unsophisticated gumshoes out of the J. Edgar Hoover
era. But the contemplative, nonconfrontational Holt,
who had been Valery Martynov's chief handler, had
worked superbly with the CIA case officer assigned to
the Courtship recruitment program. And Milburn,
who had been in counterintelligence for almost his
entire FBI career, dating back to 1978, was recognized, even at Langley, for his encyclopedic knowledge of the KGB—its institutional history, how it
operated at any given moment, what its varying priori-
ties were, how it ran its agents. There had been a
famous incident in the late 1980s during the debriefing
of a source by Milburn when the source was describing
a particular KGB operational scheme. Suddenly,
Milburn interrupted, "But hadn't they changed the
setup a couple of months before?" and the source
sheepishly responded, "Yes, of course, you're right.
I'd forgotten that."

Part two of Playactor, launched several months

later, was a parallel investigation conducted at the Washington Field Office. Valued for the precision of his mind and disciplined approach to problems, forty-four-year-old Tim Caruso, chief of Russian counterintelligence analysis in Division 5, was detached from headquarters to assemble and lead a special team. Caruso looked like a no-nonsense master at an elite private school. Other agents used to joke that if he were given striped pants and a swallowtail coat, he'd be snapped up at once by the State Department.

Informed of his new assignment, Caruso instantly recalled the words of the baseball sage Yogi Berra: It was déjà vu all over again. Five years before—on a dreary, chilly November afternoon in 1986, as a bureau supervisor concerned with KGB penetrations of the U.S. government—he had been summoned to the office of Division 5's deputy assistant director for operations and told of the probable fates of Martynov and Motorin. The loss of two bureau recruits in quick succession was unacceptable. What had gone wrong? The operation was code-named Anlace, after a medieval dagger. The question, of course, was who was holding the dagger.

And for the next ten months, Caruso, two other agents at headquarters, and three from the field office had gathered daily in "the vault," a secure, soundproof, windowless room, fifteen by twenty feet, deep in the bowels of the J. Edgar Hoover Building on Pennsylvania Avenue. They stared at a big wall chart—a "murder board"—on which every variance in the handling of the two KGB officers was noted and cross-indexed. They pored over the day-by-day records, beginning with the moment each had been targeted and recruited. They examined the circumstances of every clandestine meeting.

Presentations were made. What about this or that? Many operations involving recruitments held the seeds of their own destruction. Perhaps that was why these had been compromised. Was the FBI at fault? Had somebody screwed up? Had the cases been sufficiently compartmentalized? Who had access to them? What about the safe houses? How frequently had they been used and swept? Maybe there'd been a technical penetration by the opposition—a bug or a tap, a communications intercept—or had it been human? Was it bad tradecraft that had inadvertently pointed a finger at Martynov and Motorin? Or had they brought this on their own heads by not conducting themselves properly at all times?

There were complications. The phone call Motorin had made to his girlfriend in Washington threw everyone off. Not till the following summer was it discovered to have been KGB trickery.

There also was Edward Lee Howard to brood about. Howard, practically on the eve of his 1983 departure as a new case officer in the CIA's Moscow station, having already been briefed on a whole range of highly sensitive secrets, including agency assets in the Soviet Union, was given a final polygraph that revealed him to be a drug addict suffering from severe alcoholism to boot. The CIA not only summarily discharged him, leaving a disgruntled, troubled loose cannon to bounce around without an income, but neglected to tell the FBI about his obvious potential to do damage. Apparently, owning up was just too embarrassing.

It wasn't until the defection of KGB colonel Yurchenko in 1985 that the bureau discovered that someone answering to Howard's description was volunteering information to the Soviets and immediately placed a videocamera outside his residence in Santa Fe, New Mexico, where he'd found employment with the state legislature. Unfortunately, Howard, who had received rigorous training in detecting and evading surveillance, managed to escape past a young and inexperienced local FBI agent monitoring the camera by replacing himself one night in his car with a dummy. The next anyone heard of Howard, he was safe in Moscow. While the FBI could rightly protest that it had not learned about him until the last minute, and even then did not have enough prosecutable evidence to make an arrest, the episode remained a bitter humiliation.

But Caruso's Anlace team concluded that although Howard might well have given away Valery Martynov, he would not have been aware of Sergei Motorin. Howard had been thrown out of the CIA before the cooperation of "Meges" was made known to Langley.

Other imponderables surfaced. Around that time, a marine guard at the U.S. embassy in Moscow, Corporal Clayton Lonetree, was believed to have been seduced by female Soviet agents and had allowed KGB operatives to roam freely through the embassy after hours, even in the classified communications center. As it would turn out, while Lonetree and another marine guard might have broken the rules by consorting with comely Russian women, there was no proof that they had opened embassy doors to anyone.

Beyond this, there were unsettling confirmed revelations that had to be considered. The KGB had managed to plant electronic listening devices all over the U.S. embassy. And there was still another worry. Had national security codes been broken?

In September 1987, the Anlace investigators produced a report that recommended some tightening up of internal FBI procedures. It said that one compromise could possibly be laid to Howard, but the other couldn't. The situation at the embassy in Moscow remained up in the air, but the gut feeling was that a human penetration had occurred—and it wasn't in the FBI.

That left only one other viable candidate—the CIA. But while the agency indicated it also had been hit with source losses, the details were sketchy and no major alarm bells were heard clanging from Langley. For sure, the FBI could not investigate the CIA on its own, and it wasn't being invited in—not then, anyway.

Now, almost five years later to the day, on the afternoon of November 8, 1991, the weather outside again bleakly overcast and chilly, Caruso was back in the office of the deputy assistant director for operations. Also present was his section chief, Ray Mislock, and Bear Bryant, the new boss of the Washington Field Office.

Caruso was told that he had been selected to go over to the field office to look at multiple espionage allegations. It would be up to him to choose his investigators. He would be given a completely free hand. The fact of the matter was that there had been a huge penetration of the CIA, which had resulted in many compromises and executions. It was clear beyond doubt that the losses the FBI and CIA had suffered were due to this penetration. And it had to be human. There had been such rapid takedown of sources by the KGB that tradecraft mistakes, as well as technical penetrations, could be all but eliminated. They simply could not have happened in such a concentrated time frame in so many places. The CIA was prepared at long last to cooperate fully. A joint bureau/agency task force was already in place at Langley, attempting to identify mole candidates for Caruso to follow up on. How did he feel about it?

Tim Caruso was not overjoyed. He was on a career path in the FBI destined to lead to a top managerial slot in one of the bureau's major field offices, and he'd been around long enough to know that once he was removed from headquarters, it could easily become for him out of sight, out of mind.

He tried a lighthearted response. "You know, it's kind of funny," he said. "Just five years ago, I was in this same room, same chair, same weather, same situation."

Nobody laughed.

Then Caruso got serious. He knew that he couldn't say no thanks and walk out, but he wanted to ensure that there was no expectation something like this could be cracked in a couple of months. "I'm gratified by your confidence in me," he said. "But these investigations and analytical work can be very unsatisfying. Most of the time, they don't come to a definitive resolution. And at any rate, they take a long time. Maybe there's a lot of early enthusiasm and momentum, but inevitably it starts to wane. I know. I've been there. So I have to know that I'm going to get consistent support."

Everyone, of course, assured him that he could count on it. But it was Bear Bryant's presence that especially encouraged Caruso. Even though Bryant's background in organized crime was foreign to Caruso, word had gotten around about the Bear, his tenacity, his all-out support for his troops. Caruso had heard that he never shied away from tough decisions or hesitated to buck the system. Even though he was a boss, he still had the brio of a street agent. And on this venture, Caruso would be working in Bryant's domain, the Washington Field Office.

Also, he was heartened that headquarters had assigned Jim Holt and Jim Milburn to be the part of Playactor at the Langley end. He had great respect for both of them. Holt actually had been a member of the Anlace team, and Milburn, with his peerless expertise about Soviet intelligence, was continually consulted. Caruso had a pet name for them—Jim Squared.

Still, walking back down one of the long corridors at headquarters to his own office that November afternoon, Caruso could hear the mocking echoes of his footsteps. After all, while Anlace had exonerated the bureau of Soviet penetration, it was basically a negative conclusion. There had been no fabled smoking gun. A murderous mole was still out there.

By January 1992, Caruso had put together members of the Playactor team he wanted. They began gathering in room 11610 at the field office, another dreary, windowless, soundproof facility requiring special passes, which had been previously occupied by the special counterintelligence squad that had come up with the Libyan connection in the 1988 terrorist midair bombing of Pan Am flight 103 over Lockerbie, Scotland.

While Holt and Milburn and their CIA partners at Langley were laboriously winnowing out possible suspects, the agents under Caruso, armed with the new CIA details about Soviet "roll-ups" of U.S. intelligence assets and sources, started reviewing old unsolved cases, with all their inherent ambiguity, seeking to button them up, seeking commonalities or spin-offs that might have led to a disaster of such monumental proportions, trying to resolve years of cancerous penetration.

Caruso's crew had a new ally, the collapse of the Soviet Union and the breakdown of its social contract with the citizenry. By 1991, to use an American metaphor, nobody in what was now called the Russian Federation knew where next month's rent was coming from, what the bread-and-butter security of one's family might be. And the old KGB—reorganized and equipped with a new set of initials, SVRR—was not immune. New name or not, it was composed of the same basic personnel. Caruso saw this as a very vulnerable, quite exploitable situation. So an all-out effort was launched to pinpoint individuals who had the capability of passing on information directly or indirectly, who would either agree to a one-night stand or be willing to enter into a longtime covert relationship.

Meanwhile, a new member was added to the Playactor group at Langley (the CIA code name for it was Skylight), an agency financial analyst named Dan Payne. Payne's task was to look into the personal monetary history of various subjects on the suspect list being compiled. One name especially had attracted attention. On the face of it, his salary could not begin to justify buying a home for a large sum—in cash—in an affluent section of North Arlington, Virginia, not far from CIA headquarters. Nor was he independently wealthy. While the agency had been aware of the house purchase for some time, conventional wisdom was that it came about because of an inheritance from his wife's late father. Others had argued that no one up to this sort of treachery would possibly call attention to himself in such a brazen manner, violating, as it did, every rule of covert treason. Everyone, it seemed, had forgotten the child's fable about the emperor who had no clothes.

The FBI, without officially opening a case, could not delve into someone's bank records. But the CIA, in an exemption accorded it under the Right to Financial Privacy Act, was allowed to examine banking transactions of its employees. With the FBI's approval, Payne then sent confidential letters invoking national security to banks and credit card companies that the subject was known to use.

The upshot was startling. There were scores of deposits dating back to 1985 in two Virginia accounts that the subject and his wife had, all in cash and all, except three, below the ten-thousand-dollar currency transfer limit that banks were required to report to the

Internal Revenue Service. Large wire transfers to the
Virginia accounts were also traced to a Swiss bank,
and credit card use was found to be extraordinarily
active.

Apprised of this, Tim Caruso's field office investigators unearthed old videotapes that showed the subject visiting the Soviet embassy in Washington as a
CIA counterintelligence officer as well as tapped
phone calls he'd made to arrange meetings with Sergei
Chuvakhin, a Soviet diplomat specializing in arms
control. They were then able to dovetail cash deposits
in 1985 and 1986 that had come on the heels of these
encounters with Chuvakhin.

Further, one of the Playactor squad agents, Dell
Spry, pursuing the credit card expenditures, discovered that the subject had flown via American Airlines
to Bogotá, Colombia, and then to Caracas, Venezuela,
in October 1992. From Langley, Jim Milburn confirmed that the trip had gone unreported, contravening
a sacrosanct CIA regulation that no officer could travel
abroad without first notifying the agency.

By December 1992, for Bear Bryant, it was
enough. Throughout his career investigating organized
crime, the dictum had always been to follow the
money trail. And here it all was, as good as you
could ask for. Besides, Bryant had another problem.
Caruso's squad was now basically on hold, waiting for
a final analysis report from the joint task force at
Langley, a report that everyone had thought would be
ready months ago. And some key agents Caruso had
picked were on temporary duty from other field offices
around the country. They'd been in Washington away
from their families for almost a year. It was getting
near Christmas, and not unreasonably, with little to
do, they wanted to get home, to resume their normal
duties. Bryant could see the team drifting away right
in front of him.

But the CIA dug in its heels. It wanted a hundred percent accuracy on this one. The agency had experienced egregious transgressions in the past. A former CIA officer, while stationed in Indonesia, had sold agency secrets to the Soviets. A former low-level employee sold the blueprints for a spy satellite. A Czechoslovakian "defector," hired on as a translator, turned out to be a double agent working for Czech intelligence. Another translator, Chinese, who got top-secret clearance after becoming a U.S. citizen, had been feeding data to Beijing during his thirty-three years of service. And, of course, there was Edward Lee Howard. But nothing began to match the magnitude of what was currently at stake.

And the agency was still experiencing a terrible hangover from the machinations of James Jesus Angleton, its onetime chief of counterintelligence. For twenty years, Angleton spearheaded a crazed mole hunt within CIA ranks. At one point, he was even caught muttering that a director of the agency himself was in the employ of the Soviets. Angleton never did find his mole, but in his paranoia he succeeded in wrecking the careers of several innocent agency officers that eventually cost the CIA substantial sums in recompense. Dismissed finally, he died in 1987, and while he might now be chortling in his grave, he left an enduring legacy of shattered morale.

To Bryant's dismay, FBI headquarters went along with Langley's wishes. And even Jim Holt and Jim Milburn were counseling caution. While the suspect list was being whittled down, there were other candidates who could not be ignored.

"I should have pushed harder," he told his assistant special agent in charge of the field office, John Lewis. "I should have raised more hell."

Lewis, with his lengthy counterintelligence background at both FBI headquarters and the field office and his intimate knowledge of the way the CIA operated, replied, "Look, sometimes there are institutional mind-sets you can't overcome. It's like fighting city hall. You'll see, in the end it'll work out."

In mid-March, a draft report at last came in from the Playactor/Skylight team. There were five final suspects. One appeared to be the most likely. The problem was, though, that the other four still couldn't be definitively counted out.

Then, suddenly, the probes that Caruso's squad had been making elsewhere paid off. They brought one of the five right to the top of the list. It wasn't a hundred percent, but it was about as close as you could get.

He was, indeed, the purchaser of the North Arlington house. His name was Aldrich H. (Rick) Ames. Then fifty-one, he had worked for the CIA for thirty-one years, occupying a number of very sensitive positions. His late father had been a CIA officer before him.

With the blessings of headquarters, Bear Bryant officially opened the case on May 12, 1993.

The assumption had always been that Tim Caruso would continue to head up the investigation. But Caruso had a telling argument for why he should return to headquarters. "I'm living in somebody else's house," he told Bryant. "From now on everything should be run entirely by the field office with a straight chain of command. John Lewis is number two here. But if I stay, I'll still be reporting directly to you and taking large chunks of John's personnel that he won't have any authority over. You can't operate that way effectively and efficiently."

The Bear agreed.

The question was who should replace Caruso in leading a new squad. "It's not who the best supervisor

is," he told Lewis. "They're all good. Who's best
suited for this particular job?" He was thinking of Les
Wiser, he said. At thirty-eight Wiser was the youngest
squad supervisor in the field office, but he was a
ringwise CI agent with lots of energy who understood
the rules of evidence. He had a law degree from
the University of Pittsburgh and had been both a
prosecutor and defense attorney in the navy before
joining the FBI. Even physically, Wiser represented a
new breed of FBI agents. A slender six-footer, he
sported a big brown mustache, which, however neatly
trimmed, would have been unheard of in an earlier
time.

Lewis seconded the motion. He'd spent a week
with Wiser in Germany, just the two of them, on a
case that involved working closely with the CIA and
came back singing his praises about the manner in
which Wiser had conducted himself.

So late in the afternoon, May 24, Bryant called
Wiser to his office and told him to shut the door. The
Bear got up from his desk and paced the floor. He
asked Wiser, "Do you know what they've been doing
in the old Pan Am 103 room around the corner?"

Wiser replied that he knew something was in the
works. He'd heard the code name Playactor bandied
about. But beyond that, he knew nothing more and
hadn't tried to find out. It wasn't any of his business.
He figured that if he had a need to know, he would be
informed soon enough.

It was exactly the answer Bryant wanted. "We
have a significant penetration of American intelligence, in the CIA," he said. "We're not absolutely
certain, but we're pretty sure we know who the guy is.
It's maybe the most important case the bureau has."

Wiser felt the tingle in his spine.

"Would you be interested in running it?" Bryant
asked.

"Boss," Wiser said, "I've been waiting my whole career for something like this."

While there would be a few spillovers from Caruso's team, Bryant said, Wiser was free to pick any agents he wanted from the CI squads in the field office. Caruso and Mike Anderson, who had sacrificed an acting supervisor's job to work with Caruso, would fill him in.

Early the next morning Wiser had to go to Connecticut with one of his squad case agents. The recruitment of a source in a third-world intelligence service was on the verge of fruition and the meeting couldn't be put off.

Then the next day, a Wednesday, May 26, Wiser got his initial briefing from Caruso and Anderson. He was shown a photograph of Ames.

Looking at it, Les Wiser couldn't help a satisfied, inward smile. Ames's squinty eyes, angular face, and pointy nose made him look just like a mole.

2

Valery Martynov and Sergei Motorin were doomed the moment one December day in 1982 in Mexico City when Rick Ames, then forty, was introduced to a thirty-year-old Colombian woman named Maria del Rosario Casas Dupuy.

They had a lot in common. Neither of them was what appeared on the surface. And at the time, they had a desperate need for one another. Each could fill a special void in the other.

Rick had been assigned to the CIA's Mexico City station about a year earlier. He had diplomatic cover as a State Department political officer. Rosario arrived in the Mexican capital the following spring as the cultural attaché at the Colombian embassy.

By no means a beauty, she still retained a fresh, gamin-like quality. She was, as people said, "cute." She came from a well-known Bogotá family notable for its intellectual pursuits. Her father was a politically active former university rector and mathematician who was widely recognized for his honorable service as a state governor and in the Colombian senate for the middle-of-the-road Liberal Party. Rosario grew up on Bogotá's fashionable north side, where her mother, Cecilia Dupuy de Casas, far more flamboyant and leftist leaning than her father, presided over a salon regularly attended by academia and musicians, poets and writers, including Nobel laureate Gabriel García Márquez. While her mother was an outspoken supporter of Fidel Castro—and chaired the local Friends of Cuba chapter named after a Castro icon, José Martí, the poet leader of Cuba's 1895 rebellion against Spain—Rosario herself, except for a brief Maoist fling that was then all the rage among university students, was essentially nonideological. If there was a consistent political flavor in her life, it was an anti–North American bias, not unheard of in her milieu.

Her passion was literature. She graduated summa cum laude in the Department of Philosophy and Letters from Bogotá's University of the Andes—with a one-semester break at Princeton University in what seemed to have been a futile effort to break away from a love/hate relationship with her dominating mother, who had begun attending classes with her. Her senior paper was "The Recreation of the City in Baudelaire, Eliot and García Lorca."

Fluent in French, German, English, and classical Greek, she joined the faculty, teaching courses in literature and language, while working on a thesis titled "Esthetic Problems in Hegel with Respect to Literature" toward a doctor of philosophy degree. Administrators at the university considered her a dedicated instructor, smart, disciplined, reserved, even austere. She was to all intents the complete intellectual—focused solely on matters of the mind with little regard for the material aspects of life. And virginal.

There was, however, a hidden flip side to Rosario Casas. Although her family's political and social prominence enabled her to move in Bogotá's best circles, there was no family wealth, and her mother managed to squander what little money was left after her father died. She'd gone to school with the rich, lived in the world of the rich, and wasn't close to being rich. She began to hate her father for it, to be so near to it all and yet so far away. She was reduced to living at home, and it drove her wild not to be able to buy the latest fashions being flaunted by her girlfriends, to have her nails or hair done in the chic salons they frequented, to buy the newest Cuban music and salsa tapes that everyone was raving about, to have to beg her mother for the use of Cecilia's beat-up Fiat to get to a party, to wonder where her next pair of panty hose was coming from, to be short sometimes even for bus fare to the university or lunch money.

And there was the incessant inner tension that built up in her thin body that drove her equally wild and could only be relieved sexually. She had several affairs, but they never went anywhere as her demanding nature would eventually surface, ruining one relationship after another. She was trying to recover from another broken romance when her father's old political connections came to the rescue. The president of Colombia himself arranged her appointment to the Mexico City embassy. She'd get a new lease on life.

Rosario quickly became active in the diplomatic set's never-ending round of parties and receptions. She joined the board of AMCOSAD, a Spanish acronym for the club that sponsored social and cultural events for foreign embassy personnel. At the time, Mexico City was a hotbed of international intrigue. The United States and the Soviet Union were at each other's throats in Nicaragua and El Salvador. Castro agents were up to no good all over the place. The reigning CIA director, William Casey, was convinced that Mexico itself had all the earmarks of becoming another Iran.

A CIA case officer spotted Rosario often chatting it up with another board member, an aggressive, Spanish-speaking KGB major named Igor Shurygin. The case officer, a boozing pal of Rick's and a big ladies' man, moved right in on Rosario, pitching her and bedding her in the process. In the fall of 1982, she agreed to go on the CIA payroll. It was only for a modest two hundred dollars a month. On the other hand, it was a nice chunk of disposable change in Mexico, more than enough to buy, say, a pair of Ferragamo shoes she coveted. And she didn't have to do much for it. Just report any tidbits of gossip she picked up from the Cubans and especially any remarks Major Shurygin might drop, and to allow her apartment to be used for an occasional clandestine meeting.

Her case officer now had to extradite himself from their personal relationship. Sleeping with an asset was an agency no-no. Besides, he'd learned, like past lovers of Rosario, that once the first flush of sex was over, she tended to get to be quite a pain in the ass. So he passed her on to Rick Ames, introducing them at an AMCOSAD cocktail party. She might be just what Rick needed to shape up. His marriage to his wife, who had refused to join him in Mexico, was clearly on the rocks. With his self-esteem, always shaky to begin with, at its lowest ebb, he'd been drinking himself into oblivion. Already, he'd gotten into several public shouting matches, including one with a Cuban official during which, ironically, he had decried Castro's betrayal of the Cuban people; and he'd smashed up his car in a traffic accident, so inebriated that when a U.S. embassy representative, whom he knew well, arrived on the scene after being summoned by the police, Rick kept muttering, "Who the hell are you?"

Rosario might not look it, Rick was told, but there was a lot more there than met the eye. Sex, however, was not the instant bond between them. In his small bachelor penthouse apartment in the so-called Pink Zone—an upscale tree-shaded quarter of the city with faded rose-colored stucco walls that had an ambiance reminiscent of New York's Greenwich Village— Rosario was astonished to find wall-to-ceiling shelves filled with books. Here was no uncultured ugly American. Here, instead, was someone who could converse extensively and knowledgeably with her about great literature, who could even declaim in areas she was unfamiliar with.

He could quote at length from Chaucer!

For Rick Ames, being in the CIA was a huge personal defeat. He had dreamed of one day being in the theater, of being on stage, an actor. He had no idea then that the agency would provide him with the role of a lifetime.

And he would come to loathe the CIA. Practically the only employment Rick had ever had was in the agency. He hadn't even had the usual adolescent jobs that most other suburban kids had—like mowing lawns or delivering newspapers. He'd started working for the CIA when he was sixteen, a summer stint filing records after finishing up his sophomore year at McLean High School in Virginia, right around the corner from CIA headquarters. His father, a CIA officer, got him the job. In the family, the nickname for Rick's father was "King." And he had a regal bearing, a distant man, an alcoholic, in fact, who would disappear now and again on binges that nobody ever mentioned, but he never abused Rick, or Rick's two younger sisters, never cuffed him around. Rick thought he loved him, if that was the appropriate word in a family where emotions were routinely suppressed.

As a youngster, Rick had given his father, whose name was Carleton, the autobiography of the legendary CIA director Allen Dulles. The inscription simply said: "To Dad. Merry Christmas from Rick." The word "love," or any other term of endearment, was not included. And in 1971, after Carleton retired from the CIA, Rick received a two-page handwritten letter from him in which he wrote about the ongoing cold war and the worldwide Communist threat and then ended, almost as if it were an afterthought, by saying, "Oh, by the way, I went to the doctor, and he told me I had throat cancer, but I'm not leaving any time real soon. He couldn't tell me when. It could be six months. Or a year. Yours, Dad."

Rick kept the letter. Some years later, after his father had died, he stumbled by accident over Carleton Ames's CIA personnel file. It was listed under his agency pseudonym, which Rick knew. Regardless of how close or not a son might be to his father, it was devastating to read. The chief of the CIA's station in Burma had reported, "This person has no redeeming values. I don't see any hope for this person to ever improve. I don't blame him as much as I blame our headquarters for sending this person out here." Case officers were given a numerical rating. Carleton had gotten the lowest one possible. He was also a drunk, the report concluded.

Rick was appalled. My God, he thought, how could they have written something like that? Whatever his faults, his dad was a good man. Down the line, he would remember this.

Aldrich Hazen Ames was born in small-town River Falls, Wisconsin, not far from the Minnesota border, on May 26, 1941. His father, tall and handsome, with prematurely white hair that added to his authoritative presence, was a history professor, with a special interest in the Far East, at the local state teachers college, where *his* father had been president. In 1938, Carleton married one of his students, Rachel Aldrich, a pretty Wisconsin farm girl thirteen years his junior, who was teaching English at River Falls High School when she gave birth to Rick. She never called him Aldrich at home; first it was Ricky and then Rick.

As a kid, he was never into sports because of his bad eyesight. By the age of ten, he was wearing thick glasses. He took to chess then and was quite good at it. And books. Literature was highly valued at home—if the Ames family had a common pastime, it was reading—and Rachel Ames, by all accounts as warm and outgoing as her husband was cool and distant, spent a great deal of time guiding Rick's reading habits, introducing him to authors that most boys his age in River Falls would have drawn a blank on—to Dickens, Trollope and Thackeray, Henry James and Melville. Introverted and essentially a loner, in family surroundings that placed a premium on good manners, where private feelings and thoughts were not to be intruded upon, young Rick found it difficult to reach out to others. If they reached out to him, however, he responded with some charm. It was a trait that would accompany him throughout his life.

In all likelihood, Rick would have ended up in the academic world himself, an absentminded professor in some midwest college English department, had not the CIA in 1952, just five years after the agency's creation, recruited Carleton Ames because of his apparent Far East expertise and his undeniable devotion to all that America stood for—it was a time when Wisconsin senator Joe McCarthy was ranting that Moscow-controlled Reds had subverted every level of the U.S. government. And in 1953, after he had completed training, the Ames family found itself in Rangoon in newly independent Burma in a grand house with a multitude of servants at the ready, the fragrance of an orchid-filled garden wafting through mahogany-slatted windows. It was a revelation to a kid used to cheerless Wisconsin winters. Rick developed some athletic skills—especially swimming—and learned that this new life had been brought about by the secret world his father inhabited, for Carleton had finally confided to him what the CIA was and that he was part of it. It was a secret that Rick dutifully kept from his younger sisters. Carleton's cover in Burma was that he was on a research grant for a scholarly book on Southeast Asia.

After Carleton's return from Rangoon in 1955, the Directorate of Operations, the CIA's clandestine side, put him on probation. Like all agency officers, however, he was allowed to review the damning evaluation he'd received and protested vigorously. He was a thinker, he argued, not a recruiter—the primary standard by which overseas agency case officers were judged. And the agency backed off. With no-questions-asked annual congressional appropriations, it was in the business of swelling its ranks, not diminishing them. So Carleton became an analyst in James Angleton's mole-hunting brigade and also was assigned to lecture inside and outside the agency on the perils of Soviet infiltration—a topic of conversation he would have with young Rick instead of, say, the fortunes of the Washington Redskins professional football team. The fact that Carleton was often seen in the afternoon sound asleep at his desk provoked little comment. Imbibing was not considered a mortal sin at the agency. Even Angleton himself was often hopeless to talk to after one of his three-martini lunches.

During each summer vacation, Rick resumed his CIA clerical duties. But in high school his personality underwent a `dramatic, if transitory, change. He emerged from his shell in the imaginary world of the stage, reveling in school dramas and musicals, and wound up, in the exuberance of playing other roles, being voted class wit. In the fall of 1959, he matriculated at the University of Chicago as a history major. He quickly immersed himself, however, in the theater, which was beginning to experience an exciting renewal in Chicago. Out of the university would come the famous Second City group, with such stars on the rise as Mike Nichols and Elaine May. Using student passes, he devoured every presentation he could at Chicago's four major legitimate theaters. Cabarets and local theater flourished. He plunged into university productions to such an extent that by the end of his second year, he'd flunked his required courses. Against the competition he was facing, he also failed as an actor. Still, he did not easily surrender his theatrical dreams and found sporadic work as an assistant stage manager. But attention to details was not his strong suit, and this, too, after the better part of a year, led to a dead end.

In early February 1962, he finally gave up and, defeated, returned to his family's McLean home and got full-time employment at the CIA as a clerk/typist before moving up to document analyst. At first, Rick Ames saw this as a way to finance his continuing night school education at George Washington University. Once he received his B.A. in history, however, he found no immediate job prospects other than in the agency and in 1967 was accepted into the CIA's career training program to become a case officer. Although his acting ability hadn't been up to snuff professionally, he had absorbed more than enough stagecraft to pass himself off as mature, enthusiastic, and industrious.

And to win over as well an attractive blonde a year his junior, named Nancy Segebarth, from Buffalo, New York. A graduate of Ohio's Denison University with graduate work in international relations at American University in Washington, she also was in the career training program. When they were married on May 24, 1969, in a Unitarian ceremony, she sacrificed her own CIA career (agency rules forbade husband-and-wife case officers). They moved in with Rick's parents—where Nancy soon discovered that the Ames family preferred reading to talking to one another—before he was posted that October to Ankara, Turkey, conjuring up images of great adventure.

During his first year there, settling in, Rick got very good marks from his superiors. But, like his father, he turned out to be an abysmal recruiter, unable to initiate the contacts he was expected to make. And in the next two years, his performance ratings dropped inexorably to borderline "satisfactory." Instead of the anticipated great adventure, Turkey had become a meaningless backwater. It was just like the theater, he complained bitterly to Nancy. He never got a fair shake. Now he started serious drinking, withdrawing more and more into his own world. Meanwhile, reduced to part-time administrative work at the Ankara station far beneath her talents, Nancy became increasingly frustrated, and their marriage showed early signs of ultimately irreparable fractures.

3

Tension between Nancy and Rick Ames eased off, however, when Rick returned to Langley in 1972 and was assigned to a desk job in the Soviet/East Europe (SE) division of the operations directorate in support of CIA efforts to woo U.S.-stationed Soviet officials, particularly those at the United Nations.

Almost at once, he began reversing his dismal overseas record. He wrote with style and chalked up high scores with his incisive summary reports and carefully wrought papers on strategic and tactical planning. He also had quite a knack for languages and in his second year back earned significant Brownie points by volunteering for a CIA-sponsored course to learn Russian, which made him, as strange as it might seem, one of only a handful of agency officers in the entire SE division actually able to speak the native tongue of the enemy.

Rick and Nancy moved into Reston, in northern Virginia, a model lakeside development hailed nationally for its innovative population income mix that featured apartment houses, town houses, and grander homes set in environmentally correct pastoral surroundings. They bought a town house on Links Drive in Reston's Golf Course Island Cluster for $46,000. With the help of her banker father, Nancy supplied the down payment for the mortgage.

While she harbored no special animus toward the CIA for its rules that effectively ended her agency career—she had, as she told friends, married Rick with her eyes wide open, at least in that regard—her consciousness had been raised by the feminist movement and she became a political activist, working hard on behalf of a liberal challenger named Joe Fisher against an intrenched conservative GOP congressman. When Fisher won, she joined his congressional staff.

Still, Rick had needs that were going unfulfilled. At a Langley Christmas party, he was found drunkenly copulating with a CIA secretary on an agency desk— and on another occasion being serviced orally. Neither incident got him more than a tut-tut reprimand. After all, boys would be boys. Indeed, if anything, this elevated his stature since nobody had viewed him as much of a Lothario. There were even chuckles: "Can you believe it? That sly old Rick. He sure has a side to him you'd never guess!"

Within the United States, the CIA could collect foreign intelligence so long as it did not involve covert spying on American citizens. It did this through the equivalent of FBI field offices in major cities that were then called FR (for Foreign Resources) stations. And in August 1976, his career revived by his excellent desk work at Langley, Rick Ames was sent back to CIA front lines at FR/New York.

Nancy debated about making the move. But the idea of remaining by herself in Reston had little appeal. After she arrived in New York, a friend told her about an opening for an analyst in the State Power Authority. She noted in her résumé an impressive credential—

that she'd been an analyst in the CIA—and she got the job, later rising to a managerial position.

She made it clear to Rick that she wanted no part of his undercover work on the UN diplomatic circuit, no accompanying him to receptions and cocktail parties, which she presumed would be a duty requirement. She wanted, she told him, to lead a "normal, open life."

Rick took an apartment not far from the United Nations at 400 East 54th Street in Manhattan for five hundred and eight dollars a month, most of which his CIA housing allowance covered. Nancy came up shortly afterward. She had tried to sell the Reston town house, but there was a depressed real estate market. She couldn't get the price she was asking for, so she rented it.

And in New York, Rick lucked out on two counts. At Langley, his generally unkempt appearance, careless dress, and yellow-stained teeth from chain smoking the Benson & Hedges cigarettes he favored had not earned him many admirers. But his immediate New York boss, Rod Carlson, didn't seem to be bothered a bit by any of this. For him, Rick came off as an intellectual with more important things on his mind than grooming, which wasn't a bad quality to have when you were debriefing a source, trying to get the information you wanted. In fact, Carlson was more amused than anything by this odd duck who had arrived on the scene, and the two got along famously, often knocking down a few belts after a day at the office.

Even better, Carlson did not task Rick to recruit assets. Instead, he assigned him to handle two sources already in the fold, meeting them in agency "safe house" apartments. One was a grave responsibility, the most important Soviet government official ever to defect to the United States. His name was Arkady

Shevchenko, and when Rick was debriefing him, his cooperation still unknown to Moscow, he was undersecretary general of the United Nations. The other was a midlevel functionary in the UN's disarmament division, Sergei Fedorenko, whose familial connections (his father, an ambassador, had been head of the Soviet mission to the UN) gave him access to a range of secrets someone in his position would not normally have had.

Cheered on by Carlson, Rick received deservedly top-flight marks and promotions, diligently educating himself on what questions he should address and succinctly summarizing his reports. With Shevchenko, their rapport was helped to no end by the Soviet's taste for Scotch, which Rick was more than happy to put on his expense account. With Fedorenko, raised from childhood in the Soviet elite, it was their mutual intellectual snobbery. Fedorenko was impressed that Rick was the only handler he'd had who spoke Russian.

His marriage, meanwhile, remained one in name only. Except for the nights he was out with Carlson, or meeting with Shevchenko or Fedorenko, he was home every night—buried in his books, a tumbler of vodka by his side. Possibly once a month, he and Nancy had a night out at a restaurant. In the evening, she sometimes would go alone or with friends to a movie. He no longer expressed the slightest interest in the theater, as if he could not bear to experience what might have been. She never met Carlson or any other of his CIA co-workers. She knew of no friends he made outside the agency. In her presence, he was totally passive, completely nonconfrontational in manner. If she chastised him for forgetting some household errand, he'd just say, "I'm sorry." She handled all their finances, balancing the checkbooks. She had to remind him that his shirts were frayed, to buy new socks. She was more exasperated than angry. When he wanted to, he could be quite likable. He never mentioned his work, but he evidenced none of the resentment against the CIA that he once had.

In 1980, when a former case officer in Indonesia pleaded guilty to selling agency secrets to the Soviets for ninety-two thousand dollars, Rick told her, "I don't understand how somebody could do something like that."

A year later, he said that he was being transferred to the Mexico City station. She replied that she was staying put. He didn't argue. When he left, it was the last time she saw him in person.

Later, much later, when Nancy learned what had happened, what he was supposed to have done, she could only think it had to have begun after New York. There simply wasn't a hint of anything like it before that she could recall.

She never met Rosario.

Throughout most of 1983 in Mexico City, Rick and Rosario were inseparable. Leisurely lunches on the terraces of Pink Zone bistros, discussing literature and current events, often joined by his old drinking buddies—the case officer who had recruited Rosario and a couple of legitimate State Department types. Late-day shopping expeditions during which Rick purchased whatever clothes or jewelry struck her fancy, whether or not he could afford them, followed, as always, by torrid lovemaking in his apartment. Weekend plane trips arranged by the diplomatic club to Acapulco beaches, to the Aztec ruins in Yucatán.

Rick's affair with her got approval from his pals. Usually getting together around noon, they all drank too much—especially a deadly concoction that included tequila, rum, and beer—but Rick outdid them all, on more than one occasion barely able to make it back to his apartment, much less his embassy office. Rosario, though, made him cut down. She was good for him, they agreed. He was starting to straighten out. They had all heard from him how lousy his marriage was, the bad wife back in the States.

In attempting retrospectively to figure out what made Rick and Rosario bond, an FBI analyst said, "It's really mystifying, since neither was forthcoming in any meaningful way about how they related to one another—the dynamics of it, what drove it. In many respects, he's an emotionless person, but when it comes to her, it's different. There's a perverse need he had for her and she fulfilled it. He'll well up emotionally about her, and that's about all he wells up about. Of course, at that time, when he met her, she was a lot more attractive physically. He was suffering from incredibly low self-esteem, having lost in effect one woman, and at his age was in sort of a midlife crisis. Then along she comes, breathing new life into him both sexually and intellectually. And between the boozing and losing his first wife and sense of worth, she made him feel he was somebody again, that here was this woman from a foreign country that he could have a great passionate time with and a great career. And she had her own agenda. Down in Mexico, they were living in never-never land. She comes from a refined, prominent family, but no money, and now we're talking about moving to America and going to American universities and living in Washington, D.C., and that was a very exciting prospect. I think he masked the reality of his financial situation, and all at once she's here, wanting to do things, buy things, travel, and so forth—and what does she find? A pad with hardly any furniture near a commercial strip in northern Virginia and a ten-year-old Volvo to tool around in. That wasn't what she had in mind. He was like a puppy who'd do anything at all to please her.

Anything! And he did. It probably thrilled him. You talk about being pussy-whipped, Lady Macbeth. I'm not saying that right off the bat she knew where the money suddenly started coming from. But she wasn't stupid. She had to know at some point something was wrong. She just chose not to know. The important thing was that the money was there. That's all she cared about.''

In Mexico, Rick's assignment was to target Soviet sources and to set up a counterintelligence program. Once more, his recruitment marks were mediocre, but the overall record of the Mexico City station wasn't much better, failing, among other things, to predict the 1982 nationalization of the Mexican banking system. The biggest rap against him was allegations of his alcohol dependency, but a security office investigation concluded that while he was a social drinker who sometimes went overboard, it wasn't a major problem.

In late 1983, ordered back to Langley for reassignment, Rick told Rosario that he couldn't live without her and wanted to marry her. In Washington, he moved in for a while with a sister and her army officer husband before renting in a high-rise in Falls Church, Virginia. Rosario arrived two months later and at once Rick discovered that love really didn't conquer all. One look at where he was living and she was ready to head home. Something on the order of quaint Georgetown was what she'd expected.

At the time, Rick's CIA salary, which he did not disclose to Rosario, was $47,070.40. He explained that he was temporarily strapped because of the support he had to provide Nancy, including the rent on her apartment, which was not true. To appease Rosario, he took out a loan for a new Honda Accord while she ran up some $13,000 in credit card purchases to refurbish the Falls Church place and thousands more for clothes and endless telephone calls to Colombia and Mexico. For fear of losing her, he did not dare say that there were limits to what they could afford and that they had to live within a budget.

Rick was never one to have an unpleasant face-to-face encounter if he could avoid it, so in March 1984, during a long-distance phone call he made from Washington, Nancy got the news that he was deeply in love with another woman and desired a divorce. She knew he was back in the States through an earlier phone conversation, his voice slurred, in which he'd said there wasn't any reason for them to see each other since they had not had a "marriage" for years. She replied that she wouldn't stand in his way and hoped that at long last he would find happiness.

A month later, Rick got around to telling the CIA of his marital intentions. While marrying a foreign national was frowned upon, the rules against it were not rigidly enforced. Besides, as he pointed out, his betrothed had been a paid agency asset and intended to become a U.S. citizen. A background check commenced, which indicated that Rosario was descended from a "prominent, wealthy Colombian family." She passed a polygraph that August, at which time the CIA reminded Rick, in writing, that it might be a good idea to obtain a divorce before proceeding with the marriage, an item he'd neglected to follow through on. And at his behest, after another phone call, Nancy initiated a divorce action on September 19, 1984.

Rosario wasn't too happy to learn that under New York State law, it would take a year before a final decree was handed down. To mollify her, Rick, who by now had a range of credit cards—American Express, Visa, and MasterCard, as well as a variety of local accounts, to spread out his debt load—took her to the local Bloomingdale's to get new outfits and shoes and then to dinner at Washington's ultimate haute cuisine restaurant, Le Lion d'Or.

It was Ames's former boss at FR/New York, Rod Carlson, who finally—and unwittingly—paved the way for everything that would follow.

By the time Rick returned from Mexico City, Carlson had come down to Langley from New York and was in place as chief of the counterintelligence group in the Soviet/East Europe division. Despite the fact that Rick's Mexican tour had been considered less than stellar, Carlson remembered how well he had handled Shevchenko and Fedorenko and requested his assignment to the SE/CI group he headed. The group had four branches. One focused on counterintelligence within Soviet-bloc nations like Hungary and Czechoslovakia; a second concerned itself with the external activities of these countries; the third concentrated on the Soviet Union itself. The fourth, which Rick now ran thanks to Carlson, was tasked to thwart Soviet operations in the United States and elsewhere in the world. It was as sensitive a post as there was. Rick was in the candy store, involved in daily reviews of Soviet assets and sources that the CIA had developed, which ones might be double agents, where there was danger of a security compromise. He also had free-ranging access to the agency's global operations as well as to its tactics and strategy against both the KGB and GRU.

And he once more was getting exceptional marks—"frequently exceeds work standards" and "performance is excellent"—for his thoughtful contributions in planning new schemes, new approaches, to foil the Soviets.

Then one day, over a lunch, Carlson had an idea for Rick. Carlson said that while he was still in New York, he'd been working on a Soviet UN diplomat named Sergei Divokulski. Divokulski wasn't KGB or GRU, but he was a specialist in arms control matters, and who knew what tidbits might be picked up, where it could lead?

Divokulski had been transferred to the Soviet embassy in Washington about the same time Carlson was on his way to Langley. Carlson couldn't suddenly resume the relationship because, using a pseudonym, he had presented himself to the Soviet as a New York guy, and it might get Divokulski to wondering just what was going on.

Besides, this was a foreign resources job that should be handled by FR/Washington. Carlson said he would phone Divokulski to make the introduction and arrange a TDY (temporary duty) for Rick at FR/Washington while he continued his regular work at Langley. "It's a good deal," Carlson told Rick, "because it's operational. You'll get a lot of points for the extra effort you're making instead of sitting on your duff all day behind a desk. Stuff like that doesn't go unnoticed."

Anxious to please Carlson, if nothing else, Rick contacted Divokulski, using the alias Richard Wells. To whet Divokulski's interest, he said that he was on the intelligence staff of the National Security Council and suggested that they meet to discuss mutual security matters. It could benefit them both.

Rick began lunching with Divokulski every month or so. He faithfully reported each meeting to both FR/Washington and Langley.

In November 1984, he was temporarily detached from headquarters and was sent to New York with two other counterintelligence officers to help handle the influx of Soviets arriving for the fall opening of business at the United Nations. They were all to stay at a CIA apartment that was large enough to be used for covert meetings. But Rosario went into a hysterical tirade when she learned that Rick was going to be in New York City for at least three weeks without her. Rick caved in instantly. He not only took her along, but bedded down with her in the safe house. A female CIA officer at FR/New York, Janine Brookner, enraged by this egregious breach of security, sent off a stinging message to Langley. But all Rick got was another tut-tut for "bad judgment." The upshot was that he had to move out of the apartment with Rosario and into a hotel—at CIA expense.

(Ironically, Brookner herself would later receive treatment from the CIA that was a lot less kindly. In 1991, as chief of station in Jamaica, a rarefied slot for a woman, she was accused by subordinates—who apparently did not cotton to what they considered her high-handed manner—of being a drunken vixen who made it a practice to sexually harass male officers at the station. An agency inspector general's report confirmed the accuracy of these charges. Brookner was denied a previously offered post as chief of station in Prague and was placed in desk-bound limbo at Langley. In July 1994, she sued. All of a sudden the allegations against her began rapidly unraveling and the CIA ended up settling with her for $410,000.)

By midwinter 1985, Rick was at his wits' end. Every day Rosario was at him. Why did they have to live in this terrible place? He had promised her that as soon as the divorce came through and his financial situation was stabilized, they'd move to whatever pleased her. Well, *when* was that going to happen? She didn't know why she had ever left Mexico. She wished she were back in Colombia. And then, after these outbursts, she would be all over him in bed.

The only real bone of contention in the divorce was how the Reston town house would be divided. In desperation, he waived all rights to it. Then he wrote to the court, begging that the proceedings be expedited. "Since the action began," he wrote, "I became engaged to marry a young woman named Rosario Casas Dupuy. We had hoped to marry during the Easter holidays, but as the divorce issues were not yet resolved, those plans had to be postponed. . . . My fiancée's family live in Columbia [sic], South America. The only time that they would be able to be present at their daughter's wedding would be in the early part of June. . . . It is very important to me and to my future wife that she be married in the presence of her family."

Meanwhile, the bills Rosario was racking up kept mounting. Rick had to borrow eight thousand dollars from a federal credit union. Rosario was already talking about doing graduate work at Northwestern University. That would be another eight thousand dollars.

He felt so inadequate. And then he saw a way out. Through Sergei Divokulski. *Yes!* He saw it all now.

He'd been having this recurring dream—a series of barrier beaches were being broken down, collapsing as the reality of ocean waves slammed into them. At a solitary lunch one day, in a rush of stream-of-consciousness rationalizations, he told himself what those barrier beaches actually meant, what the reality was. The CIA director William Casey was a dangerous zealot. The whole right-wing tilt of the Reagan administration was perfidious. All this spy business was a sick joke designed to keep bureaucrats on the payroll.

He had already met six times with Divokulski. He planned a seventh one that would be a little different. But when he called the Soviet, the news sent him reeling. There would be no seventh lunch. Divokulski announced that he was headed back to Moscow for reassignment. But don't worry, he said. He was being replaced by another arms control specialist named Sergei Chuvakhin. He'd tell Chuvakhin to look for a call from "Richard Wells."

The first two times Rick called Chuvakhin, he didn't get through. The third time he managed to speak to Chuvakhin, who seemed vague. Richard Wells? Yes, he thought he did remember Divokulski mentioning the name. He'd check his files. Call him back. On the fourth attempt, Chuvakhin said that the coming week was impossible. His appointment calendar was full.

On the next call, though, Chuvakhin said he had some free time on April 16. Not for lunch, however. Yes, all right, he told Rick, a drink at the bar of the Mayflower Hotel at four o'clock in the afternoon was acceptable. "What do you look like?" Chuvakhin asked. Rick replied that he had brown hair combed straight back and a thin mustache. He wore glasses and had slightly protruding ears. But it didn't matter, Rick said. He'd leave his name with the captain.

Rick Ames prepared two envelopes, which he intended to pass on to Chuvakhin. On the larger of the two he wrote the real name of the *rezident,* the head of the KGB at the Soviet embassy—Stanislav Androsov. He then put the second envelope inside the first one, also addressing it to Androsov, but this time he used his KGB pseudonym, which Valery Martynov had supplied after he was recruited in the Courtship program. And in this envelope, he inserted the names of two KGB sources developed by the CIA whom the agency now believed were, in fact, double agents reporting back to Moscow. Rick figured that if nothing came of this, he hadn't given away much. He further enclosed a page from the SE division directory with his name highlighted, as well as a brief history of his CIA service and some other aliases he had used in the past that might be in KGB files. He also figured that if Chuvakhin by some chance had the temerity to open the larger envelope, he would stop short when he saw the *rezident*'s pseudonym. Rick spent a good deal of time pondering exactly how much money to ask for.

He considered a hundred thousand but decided that might be reaching a little. On the other hand, twenty-five thousand was too paltry a sum. Finally, in a note, he requested fifty thousand dollars. That seemed about right, he thought, based on what the KGB was known to have offered in pitches to CIA officers for information like this.

Around two-thirty that afternoon he parked his car in a garage on K Street, a couple of blocks down from the Mayflower on Connecticut Avenue. He felt his nerves starting to get to him and went into a Chinese restaurant, deserted at that hour, and had two double vodkas to boost his courage. He clutched the briefcase that contained the envelopes. Once, while at FR/New York, he'd left a briefcase containing some classified material on a subway. It had been found and turned over to the FBI. Once again, though, Rick's charmed life prevailed, and all he got was a mild verbal rebuke. Still, the incident haunted him, especially right then.

At 3:45 P.M., he entered the Mayflower bar, gave his name—Richard Wells—to the maître d', and ordered another vodka. Time passed. It was nearly four-thirty and still no Chuvakhin. He had another vodka. Instead of being nervous, he began to get irritated. Some Soviet diplomats were famously rude, failing to keep appointments without notice. Apparently, Chuvakhin fit the mold.

At a quarter to five, Rick left the bar. Out on Connecticut Avenue, he hesitated. Abruptly, he decided that if he didn't go through with this now, he might never do it. He walked a few steps down Connecticut, turned left on L Street, continued to 16th Street, and turned left again up toward the Soviet embassy.

After another moment's hesitation, he went in.

He approached the reception desk and handed the large envelope to a man behind it, obviously a security man, who took one look at the addressee and promptly put it out of sight.

Then Rick asked for Sergei Chuvakhin. A few minutes later the diplomat, a bit huffy, appeared. He regretted the missed meeting, he blustered, but an important consideration had arisen at the last minute.

Oh, that was all right, Rick replied, certain now that Chuvakhin would never know about the envelope. He understood, he said. These things happened. He just wanted to make sure that Chuvakhin was in good health. He hoped that they still could get together and again gave him his cover-job phone number, where he could be reached when Chuvakhin had an hour or so to spare.

Rick knew that every visitor to the embassy was videotaped by FBI cameras, but on that score he had nothing to worry about. Just as he was scrupulous about reporting every meeting with Divokulski to both FR/Washington and Langley, he would put in a report on Chuvakhin. This time, however, there would be a slight variation. He'd let Langley know, so at least it would be on the record, but he was sure the report would simply be filed and forgotten. FR/Washington was another matter. Because it was an operational office, somebody in it might wonder why a counterintelligence officer had physically gone into the embassy instead of arranging a meeting at an outside site. And if Rick were ever questioned, he'd say it was an oversight. He hadn't been trying to hide anything. It was right there at headquarters for anyone to see. They could look it up.

But walking back to the K Street garage that evening, he started getting the shakes again. He turned into the Chinese restaurant and had another vodka. That calmed him. Suddenly, he was confident that this was all going to work out. It was only the beginning.

The message came some three weeks later, on May 8.

It was from none other than Sergei Chuvakhin.

When Rick called back, Chuvakhin was instantly on the phone, his voice exuding cordiality. "Why don't you come in embassy?" Chuvakhin said.

This time, that afternoon, Chuvakhin was down waiting for Rick. He led him to what the FBI called the KGB room, soundproof and bug free, impossible to penetrate. Even so, after Chuvakhin disappeared, closing the door behind Rick, the lone man standing inside raised his fingers to his lips before Rick could say a word.

He motioned Rick to sit at a conference table.

He handed him a piece of paper with typing on it and a pen. The first thing Rick read was the declaration: "We accept your offer." He would be paid fifty thousand dollars for the information already provided.

Next was a question. "Is Chuvakhin OK to use for intermediary? 'Sam' is contact name." Rick wrote, "Yes, if he's OK with you, he is OK with me."

Then he read: "We hope this is long-lasting relation. We look forward to it. Is possible? We value you."

Rick Ames again wrote, "Yes." He was thrilled. For the first time in his life, he was totally accepted, *valued!*

The KGB officer, whose name he never learned, rose from the table and extended his hand. Rick clasped it. He was escorted to the door. Chuvakhin was waiting outside.

He stopped off at the Chinese restaurant for a vodka.

A week later, on May 17, Chuvakhin met Rick for lunch at a restaurant in Georgetown called Chadwick's. They discussed arms control issues. At the table, before they left, the Soviet passed him a package. In his parked car, Rick opened it and found, rubber-banded in five stacks, fifty thousand in used one-hundred-dollar bills.

He did not tell Rosario about the cash bonanza. After all, he was supposed to have money. Still fearful that she might leave him, he'd never raised a protest about her spending habits. He continued to blame Nancy for tying up assets that prevented him from moving to better quarters.

The fifty thousand dollars did not last long. To cover Rosario's long-distance phone bills, as well as minimal national credit card payments, he deposited nine thousand dollars the next day in his checking account at the Dominion Bank of Virginia. Rosario had been after him to help her mother, whom she described as destitute, so he wired five thousand dollars to a friend of Rosario's family in Miami, where a favorable rate of exchange for Colombian pesos could be obtained. He paid in cash to settle outstanding debits at the many local department store accounts he had opened for Rosario. At Neiman-Marcus alone, it amounted to nine thousand dollars. Another eight thousand went to Northwestern University for the summer session Rosario wished to attend.

At best, he realized, he was barely afloat. It was only a matter of time before he'd be submerged again. And in the inevitable second-guessing he subjected himself to after what he had done on April 16, something else wormed its way into his consciousness that began to assume paranoiac proportions. He knew that the highly compartmentalized KGB was maybe the best in the world in sealing off individual operations on a need-to-know basis. But could he really be absolutely sure? It wasn't an abstraction anymore. Right at that very moment, in the Soviet embassy, there was a KGB major who had been recruited by the FBI in the Courtship program—who could conceivably do him in.

The CIA code name for him was "Gentile." His real name, which Rick Ames also knew, was Valery Martynov.

4

At first, it was only going to be Martynov.

Before it was finished, however, Major Valery Martynov would be only part of what would come to be known in the FBI as Rick's "big dump."

It began after Rick Ames also started worrying about Sergei Motorin, the FBI's "Meges." Motorin's CIA code name was "Gauze," as in bandaging a wound. "Gauze" was inactive in agency files. All Rick knew was that "Gauze" was an FBI recruit, a political intelligence officer in the KGB's Washington residency who had been recalled to Moscow earlier in the year. But his present whereabouts were not clear. Since "Gauze" was not included in the Courtship package, the FBI had been running him exclusively. From what Rick could gather, "Gauze" wanted nothing to do with the CIA. He could be back in Washington without the agency's knowledge. Rick appreciated the FBI's intense interest in moles and double agents, unlike the agency. There hadn't been any James Angletons in the bureau. He could not rule out the possibility, however remote, that Motorin, as well as

Martynov, might learn about him. Rick himself picked up plenty of information he wasn't supposed to have during "cigarette talk" at Langley. Who, especially someone in his spot, could say this didn't happen in the KGB? So he wasn't going to take a chance. As far as Rick was concerned, it was an act of self-preservation. He'd pass on "Gauze," along with Martynov. And he was under no illusion about the fate that the two KGB officers would meet. Well, tough luck.

From there, it snowballed.

Once he had accepted the fifty thousand dollars, there was no return. They had said they wanted a long-lasting relationship with him. Those were sweet words. There was a comforting, caring quality to them, reflecting the kind of relationship that he had yearned for from his own father and never enjoyed. And he was valued! What was the price tag on that value? He'd find out soon enough.

So he added to his list the identity of GRU general Dimitr Polyakov, who went way back, a twenty-four-year walk-in recruit for the FBI. The bureau designated him "Top Hat," and he was exactly that in every sense of the word. For the CIA, when he was handed on to the agency, he was "Accord." It is doubtful that the CIA ever had a more extraordinary source than Polyakov.

A retired FBI agent in counterintelligence choked up when he recalled Polyakov. "He was just a beautiful guy," said the agent, who was one of Polyakov's handlers. "He got to New York on June 4, 1961, little more than a month before his fortieth birthday. He lived on the Upper West Side in Manhattan, on West 95th Street, about a block from Riverside Drive, with his wife, Nina, and three sons he adored. Their names were Igor, Aleksandr, and Petre. He talked about them constantly, the future he hoped for them. He was slender, about five feet ten. He had thinning jet black hair. He told me he was already balding at thirty. He had really piercing blue eyes behind the big black horn-rimmed glasses he wore. When he came to us, he was a military delegate in the Soviet mission to the UN, with the rank of lieutenant colonel in the Red Army, running spies without diplomatic cover.''

The agent shook his head, almost in wonderment. "Polyakov gave us the best we ever had about GRU operations here," he said. "We never asked him why he was doing this. That's something you never do. You don't want to get a source to thinking about that. It could open a big can of guilty worms. But he kind of brought it up himself. He'd been a highly decorated officer during World War Two, fighting the Germans, and one day, he said, he looked around and saw all the corruption and cynicism and cronyism in the Soviet Union and said to himself, Is this what I was fighting for? We wanted to pay him, but he wouldn't take a nickel. We knew he loved hunting and woodworking, so we gave him some shotguns and a bunch of power tools, which he did accept. And that was it. We told him there was always a place for him in America if that time should come, and he said, 'You don't understand. I'm not doing this for your country, I'm doing it for mine. I was born Russian and, one way or another, I will die Russian.'

"Three years later, he returned to Moscow and the CIA took him over. The last direct knowledge we had of him was in 1980 when he was in Rangoon, Burma, and then was abruptly back in Moscow. I think there was some concern about this, but it turned out to be a heart condition. That made sense. When he was in New York, he had problems with high blood pressure. And then, suddenly, there was nothing. We heard that some analysts over at Langley were saying, 'Oh, what the hell, it just showed he'd been a double agent all the time.' Unbelievable! I can tell you, nobody in the bureau bought that.''

In 1994, recently retired (fired?) James Woolsey described Polyakov as "the jewel in the [CIA's] crown." Quite aside from the hundreds of intelligence particulars he supplied, he affected the course of history. As the onetime chief of GRU's China section, he relayed crucial documents showing that the split between the Communist rulers in Moscow and Beijing was permanent. They became one of the policy pillars for President Richard Nixon and Secretary of State Henry Kissinger in opening up China. Other reports from Polyakov indicated that throughout the tension-filled early 1980s—the era of the Star Wars initiative—Soviet military planners saw a nuclear onslaught as a no-win proposition.

Thanks to Rick Ames, Polyakov would cease to exist.

Rick also threw in another FBI recruit—a KGB captain named Boris Yuzhin. He'd been turned by the bureau's San Francisco Field Office in 1976. He arrived with a group of visiting Soviet academicians. His assignment was to cultivate contacts in the Silicon Valley as well as university research institutes. Counterintelligence agents quickly picked up on him. Yuzhin was married, and the field office set him up in an awkward (for him) situation involving a young woman. Yuzhin would later claim that the ploy hadn't been necessary. He said that the supposed hot spot of radicalism at the University of California's Berkeley campus had radicalized him in a completely different way. A barrage of questions hurled at him by students about the treatment of Soviet dissidents left him nonplussed and ashamed. When his visa expired, Yuzhin returned to San Francisco as a correspondent for the Soviet news agency Tass. He provided the FBI with the clearest view it ever had about the KGB's West

Coast operations and also was able to tip the bureau about a key KGB agent in the foreign ministry of Norway—a disaster of such proportions that the famous Soviet mole in the British Secret Service, Kim Philby, by now ensconced in Moscow, was called in by the KGB to try to plumb what went wrong. The fact that Yuzhin could do this despite the fabled compartmentation in the KGB did not escape Rick's notice.

Yuzhin was rotated routinely back to Moscow in 1983 for a debriefing. Now a lieutenant colonel, he remained there for more training. He refused, however, to take on any CIA assignments in the Soviet Union. It was too risky, he said. That was the last anyone would hear about him for a long time, because on December 23, 1986, he was handcuffed, held incommunicado, and charged with high treason. He'd been under scrutiny in Moscow, he would learn, for more than a year.

Rick Ames's murderous run didn't stop there.

He passed on the identity of a KGB officer in Moscow with the CIA code name "Cowl." "Cowl" had revealed that the KGB, in order to detect spies, was placing an invisible chemical powder on, say, doorknobs, desks, or car steering wheels, which would luminesce under a special light on a suspect's hands. An enraged Reagan White House subsequently went public with the use of this so-called spy dust, charging the Soviets with a heinous disregard of the health hazards involved.

Among others, perhaps less notable, whose lives nonetheless would soon be terminated, Rick Ames purposefully disclosed an undercover GRU operative stationed in Portugal and a KGB major in West Germany, both in the CIA's pay.

A KGB officer in Athens, Greece, turned by the CIA, was called back to Moscow and summarily executed. Rick went beyond his own bailiwick. He supplied the identity of a CIA double agent, a KGB lieutenant colonel operating on the African continent, who met the same fate. His CIA code name was "Weigh."

Rick also forwarded to his KGB masters the name of Adolf Tolkachev, a Soviet defense technical expert who for years had been supplying the CIA with Moscow's advances in the rarefied world of avionics and in submarine stealth devices. Around Langley, Tolkachev was jokingly referred to as the "man who paid the rent." Rick, however, couldn't claim full credit for Tolkachev. Edward Lee Howard, the case officer who had been fired in 1983 for blatant alcohol and drug abuse, had already given him up. Howard had learned about Tolkachev as part of his briefings before being sent to the CIA's Moscow station. Tolkachev was still fighting the charges against him when Rick's information sealed his bullet-behind-the-ear death.

One of Rick's intended victims managed to escape. His name was Oleg Gordievsky. For nearly a decade in the KGB's London residency, he had been conveying information to MI5, the counterintelligence arm of the British Secret Service. While MI5 never revealed his actual identity as Gordievsky rose to the London *rezident,* Langley eventually figured out who he had to be. By May 1985, the KGB as well had zeroed in on Gordievsky as a likely British mole in its ranks, and he was summoned to Moscow. But unlike what would have happened in the Stalin era, he wasn't summarily executed. Even in the Soviet Union, certain procedures now had to be followed in accusations as serious as this. He was taken to a KGB dacha, drugged, and questioned. He continued to maintain his innocence. He was told there would be no more overseas assignments for him for the time being, and he was placed under constant surveillance.

Then Rick confirmed what he had been doing. Gordievsky was ordered to report to Moscow Center, the KGB headquarters. Fearing the worst, he alerted the Brits. And on July 19, in a dramatic rescue, hidden in the false bottom of a van, he was spirited across the border to Finland and freedom.

Rick Ames wrapped this list, along with details of twenty of the most classified CIA operations world-wide, both ongoing and planned, in heavily taped, thick black plastic.

On June 13, 1985, during a lunch discussing various arms control prospects, he passed the package to "Sam"—Sergei Chuvakhin.

He wondered how it would be handled. If the normal routine had been followed with the first package he'd delivered, the *rezident,* after seeing what was inside, would have immediately turned the contents over to his Line KR (R for residency) section chief to be passed back to Directorate K at Moscow Center. The K directorate in the KGB was responsible for all overseas counterintelligence and internal security involving not only all the other KGB lines, but all foreign ministry personnel. No part of the KGB was more secret, powerful, or feared. Probably the embassy's counterintelligence chief would open this package directly. His name was Victor Cherkashin, a tall, dark-haired, no-nonsense disciplinarian. Rick could imagine the look on his face when he found out two KGB officers had been cooperating with the FBI and CIA right under his nose. On the bright side, though, if Cherkashin was smart, and he was, he'd realize that he would end up getting the credit for uncovering Martynov and Motorin, however late in the game. That's how bureaucracies worked, whether Soviet or American. Rick's surmises were correct. Cherkashin did review the big dump. But from then on he was instructed by Moscow Center to forward all future material sealed and unopened. And he'd also soon receive one of the highest decorations the Soviet Union could offer.

That June Rick and Nancy signed off on a property settlement. Just as he'd be~n insisting to Rosario, he elicited sympathy from his co-workers at Langley, telling them that divorce had brought him to his financial knees. "When he told his first wife that he wanted a divorce because he was head over heels in love with another woman," one of them recalled, "she responded by taking him to the cleaners. When he got back from Mexico, we knew he was pretty wiped out, money-wise." Court records showed, however, that the rent on the New York apartment, then $1,085, was being paid by Nancy, not Rick. Each was to care for his or her own personal debts. Rick's CIA salary was now close to sixty thousand dollars. For him, the most onerous parts of the settlement, if they could be so characterized, called for Nancy to get title to the Reston town house (along with the thirty-seven thousand dollars still outstanding on the mortgage) and forty-two three-hundred-dollar monthly payments starting at once. Under New York State's equitable distribution laws, she also was awarded a quarter interest in his government pension.

In July, Rick received another fifty thousand dollars in used hundred-dollar bills from "Sam," as he now thought of him. He opened a safe-deposit box. Later in the month the divorce finally came through. His wedding to Rosario was scheduled for August 10.

Suddenly, though, he had a lot more on his mind.

The news swept through the Soviet/East Europe division. On August 1, a KGB defector, possibly the biggest ever, had walked into the U.S. embassy in Rome. He was Vitaly Yurchenko, a KGB colonel, about-to-be general, who was slated to take command of all the KGB's North American operations.

He underwent an initial interrogation by a CIA officer in the Rome station, who swiftly asked the big question. Had any moles penetrated the agency? More than anxious to prove his worth, Yurchenko said that there was a former CIA officer code-named "Robert" who'd been passing information to the KGB. He didn't know his real identity, but he knew the man had been thrown out of the agency right before he was supposed to be assigned to Moscow. As soon as the Rome station chief heard this, he knew that "Robert" had to be Edward Lee Howard. Yurchenko said he'd seen a cable showing that at that very moment "Robert" was in Vienna meeting with the KGB.

And, Yurchenko went on, there was an employee of the National Security Agency (NSA) who had come to the Soviet embassy in 1980 when Yurchenko was the security officer there and sold information revealing that the NSA was intercepting Soviet military communications through a secret underseas cable tap. Yurchenko didn't know his identity but was able to describe him physically.

A message reflecting all this was communicated in coded, satellite bursts to Langley, where Yurchenko would become the responsibility of the Soviet/East Europe division. The division chief assigned a veteran counterintelligence officer named Paul Redmond Jr. to head up the Yurchenko task force. Redmond had replaced Rick's pal, Rod Carlson, as his immediate branch supervisor. There would be two debriefers, and the division chief wanted one of them to be Rick Ames. Redmond, who despised what he saw as Rick's slovenly ways, mildly protested. But the division chief overruled him. Ames, he said, had a fine debriefing track record, and besides, he spoke Russian. The word on Yurchenko's English was that it was extremely poor.

Rick and his fellow debriefer were told to dig into everything available in the files about Yurchenko. He was being flown into Washington that night, and they were to be at Andrews Air Force Base the first thing in the morning to meet the plane.

Rick swallowed hard. He comforted himself that Yurchenko had mentioned "Robert," who was clearly Edward Lee Howard, and some NSA guy. But nothing about an active CIA mole, not even his code name. Rick was sure he had one himself by now, but he had no idea what it was. And if he had to, he would just somehow talk his way out of it if Yurchenko started portraying anyone who fit Rick's profile.

He did not know—nor, in fact, would he ever know—that it was the sheerest luck that Yurchenko was unaware of his existence. Yurchenko had been in Directorate K at Moscow Center, but in March 1985, barely more than a month before Rick delivered his initial package to the Soviet embassy, he had been removed from the directorate for training to run the KGB's positive intelligence operations in North America. From then on, he'd been out of the counter-intelligence loop.

As has since been widely noted in the media, Rick was late meeting the plane. One day, when Rick Ames was a household name, the conventional wisdom would be that he drank himself into a stupor the night before, terrified that Yurchenko would step onto the tarmac, take one look at him, and say, "That's the man you want. There's your mole."

While he might have had a nip or two—after all, why should this night have been different from any other?—the truth was that he'd driven to Dulles International Airport to meet Rosario's mother, flying up from Colombia for the wedding. Her flight was hours late and it was nearly one A.M. before he got home. Then he tackled the background material on Yurchenko for the first debriefing session—it was axiomatic to get off to a fast start—before dozing off, exhausted.

And he had the presence of mind to prepare a note, a question, in Russian, to try to see if he were going to have a problem. The C-5A jet bringing in the defector landed at nine o'clock in the morning, just about when the Soviet embassy in Rome was reporting Yurchenko missing to the Italian police. Seated with Yurchenko in the backseat of the car leaving Andrews Air Force Base, Rick surreptitiously showed him the note. It said, "Is there anything you wish to inform somebody at the highest authority?" Yurchenko read it, looked at Rick, and shook his head.

The FBI's Washington Field Office wasn't informed about Yurchenko till the last minute.

Around three A.M., August 2, agents in squad CI-4, which focused on the Directorate K contingent at the Soviet embassy, were summoned posthaste to Buzzard Point. Once assembled, they were told what was happening. All twenty agents would be utilized that day, providing security at Andrews and at the CIA safe house in Vienna, Virginia, about five miles southeast of Langley, where Yurchenko would be taken. And for the debriefings.

One of the junior squad agents was thirty-year-old Mike Rochford, a parochial school product out of Chicago, whose father was a city cop. Before becoming a special agent in 1979, Rochford had been an FBI support employee doing clerical work. In 1975, the bureau sent him to school to learn Russian. After a year and a half, he was back at the field office as a translator, monitoring Soviet intercepts. At the time, Yurchenko was always on the phone as security chief at the embassy, charged with protecting its physical plant and staff. So without ever meeting Yurchenko, Rochford got to know him quite well, including the fact that he was carrying on a major affair with a woman named Valentina Yereskovsky, the wife of the embassy's first secretary and a principal aide to the ambassador, Anatoly Dobrynin.

After the squad agents were filled in and getting ready to disperse, Rochford approached his squad supervisor, John Meisten, and said, "Hey, boss, if you feel like you need some special help or inside scoop about this guy, I think I can help. I listened to him plenty and remember a lot of details about him, about his personal situation when he was here."

Then he drove to the safe house to join other agents outside on the security detail. About an hour or so later, Bob Wade, an FBI headquarters supervisor in the Soviet section, emerged from the house, walked over to Rochford, and said, "Mike, why don't you come on in? We've decided you're going to be one of the debriefers for WFO [Washington Field Office]." There would be joint debriefings, Wade said, and a rotating schedule of separate ones that the agency and bureau would conduct.

At that first session, a number of CIA and FBI personnel were milling around. When Rochford entered the room where Yurchenko was, the defector was supplying more details about Edward Lee Howard, AKA "Robert." It was the first time the bureau had ever heard of him.

But for all of Rick's apparent ease, he still retained an edge of internalized tension about what Yurchenko might possibly know about him. During a break, he was off in a corner, huddling with some SE division officers who couldn't resist taking a peek at the defector. Rochford seized the moment to chat with Yurchenko in Russian, asking him small-talk questions about his flight. Yurchenko, pleased to learn that the agent spoke his language, asked where he had learned it.

The minute Rick heard Russian being spoken, he darted over. He took Rochford aside and, glowering, said, "Listen, you're not to talk to him again. You guys in the bureau, and you specifically, are just here for security. The agency's doing the debriefings, so butt out. You could mess up this whole thing."

Rochford stood his ground. "Hey," he retorted, "maybe you've been misinformed, mister. But in case you don't know it, I'm going to be debriefing for the FBI. So if I were you, I'd cut this out right now."

Rochford was so annoyed that he reported the incident to his supervisor. A day or so after, he was told that Ames's behavior was uncharacteristic, that he'd worked well with bureau agents in some debriefings a while back in New York. At any rate, his supervisor said, Ames had been given a warning.

From then on, relations between the two, while never warm, were correct. Actually, Rick made a stab at a rapprochement of sorts. That came right after Rochford questioned Yurchenko about the local Directorate K chief, Cherkashin. Why, for instance, had Cherkashin gone to Moscow briefly a couple of weeks ago? Oh, Yurchenko replied, he was presented with the Order of Lenin. That had to be for some really big operation Cherkashin had engineered, but exactly what he didn't know. Finally, Rick could completely relax. *He* knew what it had to be for. He also now knew that he was home free.

On August 10, Rick took time off to marry Rosario.

It was a bare-bones affair in a Unitarian church in Arlington, Virginia, as befitted a man whose first wife "had taken him to the cleaners." After the ceremony, glasses of wine were served. There was no reception.

One of Rick's few co-workers present from the agency did notice Rosario's wedding band studded with seven diamonds. Rick must've gone into hock pretty good for that, he thought. Boy, what love could do to a fellow.

Rick continued to have meetings with "Sam," during which he would relay a thorough rundown on what Yurchenko was saying.

Their phone calls to one another were curt.

"Are we still on for next week?"

"Thursday would be better."

"The usual place?"

"Yes."

In August, again at Chadwick's in Georgetown, "Sam" brought three other Soviets with him. Rick could not believe his eyes. One of them was Victor Cherkashin himself, who said not a word. Just ate and regarded Rick now and then between mouthfuls as the others babbled on about arms control. Had Moscow ordered Cherkashin to "eyeball" him, to assess him personally? Or was he there simply to satisfy his own curiosity? Either way, his presence sent Rick into a surreal panic. Didn't Cherkashin know he was under intense surveillance? Hadn't that FBI agent, Rochford, just been inquiring about him? With an effort, Rick tried to gather himself together. After all, Cherkashin was no fool. He had been at the embassy for almost seven years. He knew as well as anyone that the FBI kept continual tabs on him. Rick comforted himself with the thought that extraordinary precautions must have been taken to make sure there was no FBI tail. Still, he decided not to report this meeting, even to Langley. The thought of Cherkashin being there was too unnerving. After a week, when nobody said anything, Rick stopped reporting the meetings altogether. Nobody at Langley—or at FR/Washington—appeared to notice. Nobody asked whatever happened to that Soviet diplomat he was courting.

Rick's pseudonym in debriefing Yurchenko was "Phil." Although he never forgot Rick's initial arrogance, Rochford thought he was meticulous in his questioning, very professional. And he had to admit that Rick's Russian was better than his. Yurchenko, embarrassed by his pidgin English, always stumbling, trying to find the right words, tended to direct himself to Rick rather than to the other CIA debriefer, Colin Thompson, who did not speak Russian. The same held true for Rochford, whose co-debriefer from the field office, Reid Broce, also was helpless in the language. If there was a problem, it was that Ames and Thompson often appeared to be in head-to-head competition, which had Yurchenko jumping back and forth between English and Russian. On the other hand, Broce would let Rochford take the lead, invariably addressing Yurchenko through his partner.

Even Rick's chain smoking didn't seem to bother Yurchenko, a world-class hypochondriac with one complaint after another, mostly involving his stomach.

Once, taking a walk with Yurchenko in the neighborhood around the safe house, Rochford asked him how things were going. "He was really dimed out about some of the agency guards who lived with him," Rochford recalled. "But he was quick to state that he was very comfortable with Ames. He thought Ames knew what he was doing and was glad, like with me, that he was able to speak to someone who knew Russian well enough, so he didn't have to think in two different languages."

Rick even brought Rosario—the same Rosario who one day would claim she had no idea of what kind of work her husband was doing—to the safe house, where Yurchenko prepared a boiled chicken dinner for them. This broke all the rules of tradecraft, and

Rick's Langley superiors hit the roof. But he success-fully argued that Yurchenko was getting increasingly jumpy about what might be happening to the family he'd left behind in the Soviet Union. Word that he had defected was getting all around Washington. Some-body, Rick insisted, had to demonstrate to Yurchenko that this was more than a cut-and-dried business rela-tionship, that it didn't have to be that cold, that there could be personal relationships for him in America. And on that score, in splendid irony, Rick should have been listened to. As it turned out, after Yurchenko finally redefected, Rick was right. But, of course, he had quite another agenda. He wanted to see if he might be able to pick up any tidbits, overlooked in the formal debriefings, that he could report back to Moscow. Anyone who thought Rick wasn't the coolest of customers, when he put his mind to it, was making a big mistake.

Mike Rochford would never forget just how cool Rick could be. In one of the predebriefing meetings Rochford and Reid Broce held with Ames and Thomp-son, Broce reminded everyone that in questioning Yurchenko, they had to protect some very sensitive sources. While his name wasn't mentioned, everyone there knew he was talking about Valery Martynov, still at the Soviet embassy, still meeting with the FBI's Jim Holt, whom Rick had given up two months ago. Rochford remembered how solemnly Rick nodded his agreement. "It's amazing when you think how careful you're trying to be," Rochford recalled with a shud-der, "and all the time you're telling this to a fox who's already in the chicken coop."

"Boy," Rick had said, "aren't we lucky to have this guy?"

Five weeks into the debriefings, Rick was detached from them. He was going to be assigned to the CIA's

Rome station and he was off to learn Italian. He'd requested Rome because Rosario wanted to go there. She was fed up with America. She wanted to be in a Latin country with some vibrance to it, some romance. A land with a great literary tradition, the land of Dante.

Rick was replaced by another CIA debriefer, one who didn't speak Russian. By mid-September, the major work had been completed. Now essentially in CIA hands, Yurchenko started feeling more and more like a prisoner. Colin Thompson, now in charge of Yurchenko, found him personally insufferable. Thompson didn't like being in counterintelligence in the first place. The way to get ahead in the agency was to be a case officer out there recruiting sources, not debriefing them. Thompson's best CIA memories were running covert paramilitary operations in Southeast Asia during the Vietnam War, and he yearned to be back in the field. Still, Thompson set up a secret visit for Yurchenko to his old flame, Valentina Yereskovsky, whose husband was now the Soviet consul general in Montreal. But she rejected her former lover outright. To divert him, he was then escorted on trips around the United States, including the presumed delights of Las Vegas. Little attention, however, was paid to his psychological problems, to try to alleviate them. Yurchenko grew increasingly morose. His defection had moved from inside gossip to headline news.

His financial arrangements with the CIA had been settled. He knew what Arkady Shevchenko, the Soviet UN defector, had gotten, and he wanted the same—a million-dollar lump-sum payment. In addition, he was to receive a lifetime annual $62,500 as a consultant to the agency, insurance coverage, and a car. Fed up with Yurchenko's whining, Thompson snapped, "Hey, look. We have a contract. You're here to produce. Get over it."

On November 2, Yurchenko walked out of the Georgetown restaurant where he was having dinner and into the Soviet Mount Alto compound, as Valery Martynov would soon report to Jim Holt.

Rick Ames wondered how the KGB would handle Martynov. He had gleaned from the reports of the agency debriefer working with Holt in the Courtship operation that Martynov was extremely cagey, someone who wouldn't fall for the usual recall to Moscow because of "an illness in the family." Perhaps Cherkashin had given him even more responsibility so as not to alert him, while a plan was being worked out to get him back.

Yurchenko turned out to be a convenient solution.

Like Holt, Rick watched on television as Yurchenko boarded the plane for Moscow. He saw Martynov with him and smiled inwardly at the cleverness of it all. Unlike Holt, he knew Martynov would never be coming back. But he couldn't have cared less. Right then, he had a lot more to think about.

Two weeks before Yurchenko's departure, Rick Ames had met with "Sam," delivering a thick packet of CIA operational plans and counterintelligence activities.

In return, he received another $50,000 in cash. This time, though, there was a note that caused Rick's heart to skip a beat. He was advised that two million dollars were being held for him in his KGB account, payable at regular intervals. This grand sum did not include the cash he had already received. His *value* had been undeniably established.

He already had informed "Sam" that he was currently studying Italian and would be leaving Langley for Rome, and in the note there also was a set of instructions. He was to travel to Bogotá over Christmas with his wife for an important meeting. The pretext for the trip was to allow Rosario to celebrate the holidays with her mother. To make it a true family affair, Rick also decided to bring along his widowed mother, who was living in Hickory, North Carolina.

Early in the evening of December 23, he stood in front of a Bogotá movie theater. Per instructions, he was holding a copy of the international edition of *Time* magazine.

A man walked up to him and said, "Pardon me, but didn't we meet in Paris?"

"No," Rick replied, following his script. "I think it was in London."

The man guided Rick to a waiting car. His code name was "Vlad." He was Rick's KGB handler direct from Moscow Center. On the way to the car, "Vlad" warned Rick not to speak English, so the driver wouldn't divine that he was American. If necessary, Russian or Spanish would have to do. Rick decided not to say anything.

He was taken to the Soviet embassy. Inside, "Vlad" led him into what appeared to be a study, lifted out a bottle of vodka resting in an ice bucket, poured two drinks, presented one of them to Rick, smiled at him warmly, and, raising his glass, said, "To our friendship. *Na zdorovia!*"

"Vlad" gave him an envelope containing forty thousand dollars, all hundreds, all used. "Your work is greatly appreciated," he said.

Rick said that because of his Italian language courses, he wasn't in a position to provide much information at the moment. "Vlad" replied that it didn't matter. They could wait.

The KGB's code name for Rick, "Vlad" said, was "Kolokol." It meant a bell, a special bell in a Moscow tower that was rung in the thirteenth century to warn the citizenry of the approach of Genghis Khan's Mongol hordes. He was to sign any secret communications with the letter "K."

He also said that Rick was to continue to meet "Sam" in Washington in the event anything did come up. When he got to Rome, there would be a new intermediary, a diplomat at the Soviet embassy whose name was Aleksey Khrenkov—"Sam II." Rick was not to call him. Khrenkov would find a way to introduce himself. The procedure would be the same as in Washington. Rick was to convey whatever he wished to him. He was not to discuss the contents under any circumstances. "Sam II" would pass back "envelopes."

Rick had been tossing down vodkas. He glanced at his watch. He'd been with "Vlad" for more than an hour and a half. "Oh, God," he said. "I've got to leave. I told my wife I'd only be gone a little while to do some last-minute shopping. She'll have a fit."

For Christmas, Rick proudly gave his mother a lovely emerald on a gold chain. When Rachel Ames expressed astonishment that her son could afford such a lavish gift, he confided that a friend of his had let him in on some lucrative investments. After Christmas they all traveled to the old colonial city of Cartagena on Colombia's Caribbean coast, recently rediscovered by wealthy Bogotá families, who were buying and restoring vacation homes there. The previous November, at Rosario's behest, Rick had agreed to purchase a condominium for her in the city's historic district by the sea. They also spent a night at a nearby *guajira,* a combination cattle ranch and coconut farm that belonged to a friend of Rosario's mother, Cecilia. Rick ended up contracting to acquire, for $20,000, a piece of the property, which he put in the names of both Rosario and her mother.

Around that time, in Moscow, Valery Martynov's wife, Natalya, was brought to Lefortovo prison, where for the first time since he'd left Washington with Yurchenko she saw the haggard face of her husband. He was, she was told, being charged with high treason.

"How are the children?" he asked.

5

Yurchenko's redefection left the CIA's top management aghast.

Then, when it was learned that Yurchenko not only had not been summarily executed, but had been given a new job advising Soviet embassies and consulates on security measures, Langley analysts went into an orgy of internal pretzel bending. Was Yurchenko a true defector? Or had he been a Moscow-created double agent? Was he a plant to divert the agency's attention from some other devious scheme the KGB had under way? Had he been sent to protect a mole already in place?

The agency decided it was just too humiliating to admit being taken in by someone who might have been a double agent. So in a story in *The New York Times,* an unnamed official declared that Yurchenko had become upset when the FBI showed him newspaper stories about his defection. "This is when he began thinking maybe he'd made a big mistake," the official was quoted as saying.

The fact was that the FBI didn't have to show

Yurchenko a thing. He routinely read the papers every day. Nor did the bureau believe that Yurchenko was anything other than a disillusioned defector, treated with callous indifference by the agency. He'd given away too much. Because of him, a CI squad finally tracked down Ronald Pelton, the National Security Agency employee who'd revealed to the KGB that a key Soviet underseas military link was being tapped. And Yurchenko also had disclosed one of the KGB's darkest secrets—how a deadly poison pellet imbedded in an umbrella tip was used to murder a Bulgarian dissident in London a few years before.

It seemed that Yurchenko had gambled and won, betting in the beginning that he was such a high-profile case that the Kremlin, instead of executing him, would use him to demonstrate to a watching world that the Soviet Union was a forgiving, humane society. As it turned out, Yurchenko had something far more practical going for him. The head of the KGB's First Chief Directorate—the equivalent of its CIA—had been the Washington *rezident* when Yurchenko ran embassy security. And over the objections of others in the KGB, he insisted on appointing Yurchenko to oversee North American intelligence operations. To admit now that he'd erred grievously was too embarrassing. He laid down the official law. Yurchenko, indeed, had been drugged and kidnapped by American agents and held against his will before he'd escaped. Yurchenko was even honored with a medal for his resourcefulness in fleeing his captors.

When Mike Rochford learned this, he couldn't help remembering Yurchenko's description of the KGB's inner workings, what drove its staff, about its operations, the politics and personal machinations involved—and thinking that it was all a mirror image of what went on at the CIA. Bureaucracies, whether dictatorial or democratic, had a lot of unfortunate similarities.

It was in this context—as the FBI was starting its Anlace probe under Tim Caruso to try to determine why Martynov and Sergei Motorin had abruptly vanished—that the CIA began wrestling with the alarming disappearance of some of its best Soviet sources.

The first indication of trouble was the ominous recall to Moscow of the London *rezident*, Oleg Gordievsky, whom British counterintelligence, MI5, had recruited. The CIA's code name for him was "Tickle." And MI5 made it clear that it believed the leak came from the American "cousins." Then, on June 13, 1985—the day Rick Ames made his big dump—Adolf Tolkachev, who'd been supplying the CIA with the Soviet military's most exotic scientific and technical secrets, failed to rendezvous with his case officer in Moscow and was never heard from again.

At first, once Yurchenko had unmasked him, the culprit was thought to be Edward Lee Howard. But, according to a CIA inspector general's report, it became apparent that other sudden "roll-ups" could not be blamed on Howard.

Before it was over, it became evident that the CIA's entire anti-Soviet operation was collapsing. Nothing made sense. For agency spy catchers, if the KGB had a mole inside the CIA, the rules of the game said that the last thing it would do was call attention to him by wiping out everybody he'd fingered in one fell swoop. And, as the inspector general reported, "[Our] cases were being wrapped with reckless abandon."

No one at Langley apparently shared the perception of the FBI's Caruso that when the victim of a car accident was hemorrhaging, you stopped the blood flow first and worried about the rest later. The problem was that the agency was not geared to developing evidence to arrest and prosecute a suspected traitor within its ranks. At best, its cultural know-how was to find an asset working for the enemy and to turn him around, turn him into a double agent.

The possibility of a technical penetration was weighed carefully. There was also the theory, widely subscribed to, that despite the number of cases being compromised, each might hold within itself "the seeds of its own destruction." In CIA jargon, a "case" was anyone who was providing useful intelligence whether or not he was fully recruited.

In October 1986, the CIA set up a four-member special task force to try to resolve the "compromises." While they were by no means trained investigators, they were portrayed as "seasoned officers who had operational or counterintelligence experience." Their stated mission was to consider what CIA offices had been involved in the compromised cases; which agency employees within these offices had access to the information; and how many of the compromises could be credited to Edward Lee Howard and how many others might be explained by faulty CIA operational procedures.

Reluctantly, the task force had to concede that only two, possibly three, of the compromises were Howard's doing. Later, this estimate was raised to seven more cases Howard potentially could have known about it. That still left plenty of others to explain away. Worse yet, when the task force started, it was thought that around thirty CIA operations had been given up or had run into "problems." Then, all at once, the number jumped. Senior management in the Soviet/East Europe division was informed that at least forty-five cases and two technical operations "were known to have been compromised or were evidencing problems."

Suddenly, there was great hope that alleged misconduct by two marine guards at the U.S. embassy in Moscow, Corporals Clayton Lonetree and Arnold Lacey, would fill in the gaps. The allegations against the pair were that they'd been seduced by Russian women under KGB control and then at night had let the KGB inside the embassy. The task force hypothesized that if KGB operatives were able to get access like that, they could have combed through all sorts of secret CIA records. Months were spent futilely trying to confirm that such an entry occurred. Lacey was never prosecuted. Indeed, Rick Ames was able to crow to the KGB in a message, signed "K," that the Clayton Lonetree affair was sure to draw any possible attention away from him.

Nevertheless, with the marines out of the picture, the task force in its analysis, according to the inspector general, did not create a formal list of agency suspects, nor did it initiate any specific investigations. The chief of the division's counterintelligence group was quoted as saying that CIA management, while supportive of the review, did not attach "undue urgency" to it. "People," he added, "ask me whether [my supervisors] bugged me about it. I said no, they didn't bug me about it because they don't call up their doctor every five minutes and say, 'Do I have cancer?' But we kept them informed. I mean, they did not put a lot of pressure on us, but they encouraged us. . . . The problem was that we didn't make any progress and we didn't get any answers."

By then, the CIA was aware of the FBI's Anlace probe. And in an off-site meeting with the bureau, there was a discussion about trading information. But an agency representative strongly objected to what he called the FBI's "inquisitiveness" about CIA operations and activities. Allowing that the bureau had disclosed some of its own "dirty linen," he said that nonetheless "a conscious decision has to be made here concerning the degree to which we are going to cooperate with, and open ourselves up to, the FBI." The upshot was that while the bureau was supplied with summaries of CIA compromises as they were learned, the bureau was not going to be permitted to see any detailed operational files. And the devil, of course, was in the details. The reason given was that this was standard procedure when there was no information specifying a human penetration of the agency.

The KGB, meanwhile, was throwing out one red herring after another. First, it consciously spread the word through CIA sources, already identified by Ames, that Edward Lee Howard was the counterintelligence bonanza of all time. To further confuse things, it used other sources to promote the idea that the compromises resulted from poor CIA tradecraft or the "personal shortcomings" of CIA personnel.

The KGB's most successful diversionary ploy was to have one of its officers in East Germany leak to a CIA contact that it had cracked a supersecret, worldwide communications facility that the agency had established in Warrenton, Virginia. KGB knowledge of the location alone was enough to give everyone the willies. More than a hundred agency employees worked there, and the task force spent the better part of a year trying to isolate which one among them might be the guilty party.

Based on the reports he received, Robert Gates, then CIA's deputy director, would blame the compromises mostly on tradecraft problems. Things like this happened, he said. But the real problem was that the covert elitists in the operations directorate could not come to grips with the possibility that one of their own would be in Moscow's pay. All right, there was Howard. But he was a misfit, a doper, and a drunk. And he'd been kicked out. Case closed.

The dark legacy of James Jesus Angleton still hovered over the agency.

Gradually, the concern about the compromises receded. There hadn't been any recurrence, and the agency was developing new sources without incident. The attention of the special task force shifted to an assignment ordered by William Webster, who had succeeded the late William Casey as CIA director. In the event this situation ever did crop up again, Webster wanted a new coordinating office in place called the Counterintelligence Center.

While this was going on, a security office investigator (the only one) who'd been assigned to look into a human penetration learned that an officer in the Soviet/East Europe division always had a great deal of trouble getting through routine polygraphs. What's more, the word was that the same officer was throwing around money that his salary couldn't begin to justify. This caused quite a stir, but in the end it didn't pan out. The officer's wife had come into a big inheritance.

On another front, the Washington Field Office had started making inquiries about Rick's meetings with "Sam"—Sergei Chuvakhin. After Rick was videotaped going into the Soviet embassy that first time, the field office, through FBI headquarters, immediately checked him out. Back through channels came word from Langley that Ames was courting Chuvakhin in the hope of extracting some information out of him. So Rick's second visit to the embassy at Chuvakhin's invitation—the one during which he met the KGB officer in a secure room—didn't cause any concern. In all, Rick had reported six meetings with Chuvakhin. But in a records review, the field office noted that there were several phone intercepts between Ames and Chuvakhin to set up meetings that Rick apparently hadn't reported. No great urgency was involved here. Chuvakhin had been covered by a CI squad when he'd moved from the Soviet UN mission in New York to the embassy in Washington, and it was established that he was neither KGB nor GRU, but a real diplomat, as advertised, specializing in arms control. It was just a matter of dotting all the *i*'s, crossing the *t*'s.

At Langley, Rick was asked about the missing reports. Well, he said, it was an oversight. And there really wasn't much to report, anyway. Chuvakhin had begun to look less and less like a prospect worth pursuing. He'd just been going through the motions to make sure.

Waiting for some response, a CI agent contacted the CIA's FR/Washington office to see what it had on the meetings. "Not much," the FR chief said. "He wasn't one of our guys. I mean, he was assigned to us on a TDY. We hardly ever saw him. The way I looked at it, he was a freebie. I was getting a free body. If he turned up something, so much the better. He wrote up some reports and I asked a couple of times where the other ones were. He said he'd get to it, but he never did. I figured what the hell, it wasn't that big a deal."

Then the FR chief's jaw dropped when he was told that Rick had been inside the Soviet embassy twice. He said he hadn't known anything about that. If he had, he would have raised hell. A counterintelligence officer going right into the embassy, exposing himself like that! It just wasn't done.

Now the field office, again through FBI headquarters, dispatched a much stiffer message to Langley. What was with the reports?

By then, Rick was long gone—to Rome. An agency cable came in requesting that he hop to. Rick tore it up. There was no follow-through, at least not at that time.

In March 1986, Rick got another $30,000 in cash from "Sam."

Prior to his departure for the Rome station, on May 2, he was given a polygraph examination, the first one he'd had in ten years. In Bogotá, he had asked "Vlad" if the KGB possessed any drugs to combat a polygraph. "Vlad" had said no, but not to worry. The main thing, he'd said, was to get a good night's sleep and to relax. And to connect with the polygrapher, make friends with him.

Rick tried to comply, but going into the polygraph, he was still worried and anxious. It was just over a year ago that he'd walked through the embassy gates on 16th Street after fortifying himself with vodka.

The polygrapher zeroed in on any unauthorized contacts with foreign intelligence services, on the unauthorized disclosure of classified information, and on any financial problems Rick might have.

Rick gave what were deemed "deceptive" responses to specific questions about whether he'd been pitched by a foreign service. To the polygrapher, that was odd since the subject seemed to be fine on other issues relating to counterintelligence and to the naked eye came off as quite congenial, not at all hostile or nervous. So, contravening the rules, he asked Rick what he thought the problem was. And Rick said that the idea of being pitched by the enemy always weighed heavily on his mind. Everyone knew that "the Soviets are out there somewhere" and it was foolhardy not to worry about it. He himself as a case officer in the field had made pitches, and maybe the Soviets knew about them. It was not so long ago that he'd been debriefing a KGB defector who had redefected, and it was more than possible that the KGB had a description of what he looked like. He was feeling even more unease because he was about to be posted overseas and might become a target. It was hard to explain, he said, but he was glad he'd gotten these worries off his chest. He felt a lot better having done so.

This earned him a second round on the machine. And this time, he passed with flying colors. He was found to have been both "bright" and "direct." On the record, Rick Ames was clean.

About a month after his arrival in Rome, he attended a diplomatic reception. Rick was sipping a Scotch as he observed the scene. A stranger came up to him. It was "Sam II." "Hello," the man said. "My name is Khrenkov. I have heard about you. We should get together soon."

6

In Moscow, the new leader of the Communist Party, Mikhail Gorbachev, was calling for dramatic changes in the way the Soviet Union did business—for the openness of *glasnost,* and the restructuring (*perestroika*) of the Soviet system, its *demokratizatsiya,* or democratization.

In Rome, Rick Ames was handing over shopping bags full of classified documents to Aleksey Khrenkov.

While Rick did not occupy a counterintelligence slot anywhere near as sensitive as he had at Langley, he now had an even broader range of general information coming his way—a huge paper flow not only of CIA material, but also of secret State Department cables and National Security Agency communications, all of which passed through Rome. There would come a time when some of his CIA colleagues would recall how keenly interested he seemed to be in areas that on the face of it were completely unrelated to his own work. But nobody in those days ever made an issue of this.

And just as Vienna was for the Soviets, Rome was the preferred city for the CIA as well as for U.S. military intelligence to debrief agents when they could be brought out from behind the Iron Curtain, from countries like Poland, Hungary, Bulgaria, Czechoslovakia, and Albania.

Even if he wasn't present at these debriefings, in his new posting as the Rome station chief of the "enemy targets" branch—which basically meant the Soviets—Ames knew about them, would very often arrange for the safe houses where they were to be held, and subsequently was able to pass on the locations to the KGB, which took it from there, surveilling the scene, photographing the participants. Rick knew who the agency case officers were and the subject matter of the meetings. If he didn't always know the actual identity of the sources being debriefed, he was aware of their code names and frequently had enough profile background for the KGB to pinpoint them. He attended staff meetings, held weekly, in which the value of assets in hand, as well as potential recruitments, were discussed. And he also coordinated the CIA's role in the double-agent operations being run by the Pentagon.

Rick gave the first batch of material to "Sam II" in October 1985, when he met him for lunch. He carried it out of the embassy in a shopping bag underneath some magazines and newspapers. He'd earlier made a test run limited to the publications and nobody had questioned him. Nor did anyone ever. It was just as it had been at Langley, where briefcases or packages he was exiting with were never checked.

In return, he got $50,000 in cash, half in dollars and the rest in Italian lire. The lire were for current outlays, for the maid Rosario had hired, for her shopping and constant phone calls to her mother in Bogotá. He needed it. Despite the fact that Rick had received nearly $200,000 in blood money thus far, Rosario found no trouble getting rid of it. She'd already been on one buying spree for clothes in Paris and had journeyed to Germany to bone up some more on her favorite philosopher, Wilhelm Friedrich Hegel. Undoubtedly, he would have been quite pleased with his devoted student. Hegel believed in the inevitability of dialectical logic—a thesis and antithesis combining to produce a synthesis. Rick and Rosario personified it. Rick kept the bundles of cash in a four-drawer safe in his office, drawing from it as the occasion demanded.

As he had with Sergei Chuvakhin in Washington, Rick initially reported his meetings with Khrenkov. He said that he thought they might lead to a recruitment. But he made sure to downplay Khrenkov's potential, so as not to spark follow-up queries about how the relationship was coming along. Khrenkov, as Rick described him, was the sort of person a diligent case officer ought not to overlook. You never knew when there'd be a payoff. After a while, he stopped documenting the meetings altogether.

In March 1987, "Vlad," Rick's KGB handler from Moscow Center, arrived in Rome. It had been fifteen months since they'd last seen one another in Bogotá. Khrenkov picked Rick up on a street corner. Rick was wearing a billed cap pulled low over his face. He lay on the rear-seat floor of Khrenkov's car as the diplomat drove him through the gates of the Soviet compound.

"Vlad" had a bottle of vodka ready. He toasted Rick again, complimenting him on his excellent work, reiterating the high esteem that was accorded him in Moscow. And Rick remembered that—the glow he felt upon hearing it. Unlike in Langley, or even here in the Rome station, there were no snide comments out of Moscow about his capabilities.

"Vlad" brought good news. Rick had requested payments of $10,000 a month. Instead, out of the $2 million being held for him, he would be getting $300,000 annually. And on the spot, "Vlad" handed over a hundred thousand dollars. He said that $250,000 of the money in Rick's name was in interest-bearing bonds, the remainder in regular savings. He did not specify where, nor did Rick inquire. He warned Rick about an unseemly display of his money. It invited disaster. He advised Rick that it might be wise to open a Swiss account. He recommended Credit Suisse, Switzerland's biggest bank, which handled a vast traffic in international transactions.

By then, although it remained unofficial, word had spread through the CIA's covert operations directorate that an unusual, if not extraordinary, number of case roll-ups by the Soviets were suddenly taking place. "Vlad" wanted to know if any of this had affected Rick. Downing one vodka after another—later, he'd remonstrate to himself that he had drunk too much, but the tension was almost more than he could stand—Rick replied that it really hadn't been a problem yet. The FBI had made some inquiries about unreported meetings in Washington with "Sam." A cable had arrived from Langley about this, but he said he'd ignored it, and that he'd heard nothing more. It looked like a dead issue, but, still, the sudden roll-ups, occurring all at once, had put him in an awkward position.

"Vlad" was regretful. If it had been up to the KGB, it would never have happened that way. Unfortunately the situation had been brought to the Kremlin's attention—and the shocked rulers of the Soviet Union had panicked, demanding that action be taken immediately. As a professional, "Vlad" said, Rick had to recognize that such realities existed in all governments.

In any event, "Vlad" assured Rick that the KGB was employing diversionary tactics to throw the CIA off the track. One was to lay everything on the disgraced Edward Lee Howard, who had been fired by the agency before his posting in Moscow.

That was funny, said Rick. The cover-up of Howard by the agency had been so thorough that he'd never heard of him until the defection of Vitaly Yurchenko. "Vlad" said that the Howard case showed how the KGB protected its own. Howard was meeting his handler in Vienna when the KGB learned of Yurchenko's mysterious disappearance, and he was instantly told that Yurchenko might have information pointing to him. It was this forewarning that put Howard on the alert, "Vlad" said, enabling him to escape FBI surveillance back in America.

Rick asked about Howard. Where was he? "Vlad" said that while he did not know him personally, he understood that he was in good health, living in a beautiful country house, a dacha, outside Moscow. Perhaps one day Rick and Howard would meet.

Then "Vlad" pushed him hard about any other major penetrations, past or present, that the CIA had developed against the Soviet Union.

That was when Rick decided finally to give up Sergei Fedorenko, one of the two members of the Soviet mission to the United Nations he'd been debriefing in New York before being reassigned to Mexico City. He hated doing it, but he couldn't dismiss the hundred thousand dollars he'd just been given or the rest of the three hundred thousand that would be coming to him during the year.

Fedorenko and he had gotten along well, become friends, in fact, so close that when the Soviet didn't know how to hide the payments he was receiving from the CIA, Rick volunteered to step in on his behalf. Except for his UN credentials, which he thought would be a sure giveaway if someone checked him out with the Soviet mission, Fedorenko had no other identification, not even a driver's license. Rick brought Fedorenko down to Washington and introduced him to his own branch manager of the Dominion Bank of Virginia in McLean. "Look," Rick said, "you know I work for the U.S. government"—which in McLean automatically meant the agency. "How about doing me a favor? This is a friend of ours. Would you open up an account in his name? I'll guarantee him. Use my address and just send all his statements there."

Rick told "Vlad" that Fedorenko's CIA code name was "Pyrrhic" and that the name Fedorenko knew him as during the debriefings was "Richard Altman." That was important. While interrogating a suspect, nothing made one fall apart quicker than throwing in something like "Now, tell us, when did you first meet Richard Altman?"

To handle current expenditures, Rick opened two accounts in the Italian Banca Nazionale del Lavoro, one for dollar deposits, the other for lire, maintaining balances in each ranging between ten and twenty thousand dollars.

He drove with Rosario to Switzerland, to Zurich, to open an account with Credit Suisse. By now, even Rosario was aware that Rick had money coming that was beyond his CIA income. He elaborated on the story that he'd told his mother in Colombia when he'd presented her with the Christmas emerald. He had this friend in Chicago, he said, who was dealing in large transfers of money that he was helping him out with. He said that the friend's name was "Robert." It was Rick's private little joke. "Robert" had been Howard's Soviet pseudonym.

Implying that this had something to do with trade union pension funds and the Mafia, Rick said that it was nothing she should talk about. Not that it was a necessary warning. Rosario knew what Rick's work involved. She'd been with him at dinner with Yurchenko and knew perfectly well who Vitaly was. Rosario, at best, was the classic Mafia wife. She knew, but she didn't know. She never once questioned Rick further about "Robert," never expressed the slightest wish to meet this family benefactor, having him come by for a cocktail, say, or dinner. The important thing was that the cash kept flowing in. That was all she cared about.

In Zurich, in Rosario's presence, Rick explained to a Credit Suisse representative that his wife's family had holdings in Italy that were currently being liquidated and that periodically he would be transferring the proceeds into his account. He opened the account in both his name and Rosario's.

In Rome, Rick began to lay the groundwork to explain Rosario's extravagance—the expensive designer clothes and the jewelry, rings, necklaces, and bracelets that she was wearing, the possibility that the phone bills she was running up in calls to Bogotá that he was getting at the office (as high as five thousand dollars a month) might be noted. At least twice, on social occasions where embassy personnel and staff from the CIA station were present, he spoke about the fortuitous inheritance his wife had received from her family in Colombia. At a small dinner party, attended by Rosario, he exclaimed what a lucky fellow he was. "Here I just thought that I was marrying this wonderful, intelligent woman," he said, "and all along I was marrying into money, too." As if reproaching him for his poor taste in table talk, all Rosario said was, "Rick, dear, I wish you wouldn't drink so much."

To back this up, in the event anyone ever looked

into it, Rick began a primitive form of money laundering. Rosario's mother, Cecilia, was totally dependent
on the fifteen hundred dollars he was sending her each
month. She would oblige him in any way she could. "I
need to ask a favor of you," he wrote to Cecilia. "The
Swiss authorities won't allow an American citizen to
have two accounts, which I wish to have. So therefore
I need to open an account under your name. Don't
worry, I will put myself in as trustee. You won't have
to concern yourself about it at all after that."

In Bogotá, following his instructions, she went to
the Swiss embassy, indicated that she wished to open
an account in Zurich, signed over a power of attorney
to Rick, and had it forwarded to him. He took the
power-of-attorney letter to the bank and opened the
account for Cecilia Dupuy de Casas, and from then on
the cash he was getting from the Soviets was deposited
in it first before being transferred elsewhere.

Rick kept feeding "Sam II" with bagfuls of cable
traffic, the names of double agents—some fifty of
them, all told—being run by the Naval Investigative
Service, the U.S. Air Force's Office of Special Investigations, and the Army Intelligence Command, all of
which, if they were conducted outside the United
States, had to be undertaken with the CIA's knowledge. And in Rome, Rick was liaison between the
agency and the military. Often, he would become
aware of similar operations in other parts of Western
Europe. Service investigators actually brought them
to Rick's attention to try to get the CIA more involved.
The agency generally did not like double-agent operations because it meant giving up information. But the
military loved to let an enlisted man or a junior officer
volunteer to "work" for the Russians in order to find
out what strategies the Soviets had. And the KGB
loved knowing who they were even more. It gave the
KGB a chance to lord it over its archrival in the

USSR, the GRU, the chief intelligence directorate of the Soviet General Staff.

In return, Rick got the money. The payments averaged thirty thousand dollars, some of it in lire. In July 1987, one bundle was in West German marks. Every so often, as the cash accumulated in his office safe, Rick deposited it in his mother-in-law's Credit Suisse account. So as not to leave a trail, he never wired it. Instead, he always carried it personally, usually traveling by plane. The flight was less than two hours, so he could be gone and back in one day. And, of course, he never reported these trips out of Italy as CIA rules required.

In December 1987, "Vlad" reappeared in Rome. Rick always saved something special for his KGB handler. This time it was a Bulgarian intelligence officer. He'd been a walk-in. Unfortunately for him, he'd walked right into Rick Ames. Bulgaria wasn't that large on the CIA's scope. Still, the Bulgarians were aggressive and often up to no good, far more prone, for example, to engage in "wet work" than other Soviet-bloc nations, as in the poison pellet murder of the Bulgarian dissident in London. And there'd been the attempted assassination in Vatican City of Pope John Paul II. Although the shooter was a Turk, three members of the Bulgarian security service were implicated in the conspiracy (with the KGB a shadowy presence) and went on trial in Rome. Only a year ago, they had been freed for lack of evidence, but suspicions lingered on and the matter was never fully resolved. Perhaps this walk-in could shed some light on it, among other items. He was nervous, however, about being in Rome, so arrangements were made for a subsequent meeting in Athens.

To the surprise of everyone—except Rick—he never showed up.

At Credit Suisse, he also opened a corporate account in the name of Robeco—another bow to "Robert." The idea was to funnel money into it for investments. But it never really got off the ground. As fast as the cash arrived, Rosario found ways to spend it. Rick asked "Vlad" if a million dollars of the money being held for him couldn't be put into a Credit Suisse account solely for investment purposes. "Vlad" said he'd look into it, but he did not think that this was possible. It was the only time a request of Rick's wound up being rejected.

During their first year and a half in Italy, he and Rosario found their stay rather adventurous, even romantic. There was nothing shabby about where they lived, at 10 Via Vincenzo Bellini, named after a nineteenth-century composer of operas, in a quietly rich quarter close by the famous Villa Borghese gardens. And Rosario delighted in her trips to France and Germany, others to London and Madrid. Rick and she toured the ruins at Pompeii and vacationed in the picturesque jasmine-scented village of Positano south of Naples on the Bay of Salerno. At Christmas, at Rosario's urging, he picked up the tab for Cecilia to visit them.

Gradually, though, things began to change between them.

The stress of what he was doing had finally begun to get to him. Turning over Sergei Fedorenko weighed on him more than he had imagined. It had seemed so easy at the time. He had not seen Fedorenko for years. He'd become almost faceless, like the others. But the memory of him, their talks in the New York night, had returned to haunt his dreams. "Vlad" never mentioned what had happened to him. He didn't ever mention what had happened to any of the names Rick had betrayed. But like nearly everyone in the operations directorate, Rick knew about the fate of

Martynov and Motorin. And there was the Bulgarian. Rick couldn't have cared less about him, but he wasn't a cipher, either. He was a live human being whom Rick had spoken to, actually had shaken hands with. He wondered what Mafia hit men felt like. He had read that they never considered that anything personal was involved. Just another workday chore. Well, what the hell. As he brooded about all those he'd given up, he told himself that they took their chances and he was taking his.

He reverted to the heavy drinking of his days in Mexico City before meeting Rosario. These were solitary binges. Once he was found passed out cold in a Rome gutter by the Italian police.

As if to bolster his ego, he indulged himself for the first time. He had his teeth capped. And he discarded his nondescript jackets and trousers for Armani suits.

His marital relations started deteriorating. Rosario was not aging gracefully. Her nose had become more prominent, and dark circles were forming permanently under her eyes. Rick once remarked that perhaps she should put on a little more weight. In a city of voluptuous women, it was the wrong thing to say. Oh, so that was it, she screamed at him. She was too skinny.

He assiduously avoided further confrontations. It had never been his nature anyway to be combative, either with Rosario or his first wife, Nancy. Faced now with Rosario's incessant demands and hysterical outbursts, he increasingly retreated into a passive stance. Combined with his drinking, he grew indifferent to sex, unresponsive for the most part to Rosario's best efforts to rouse him. When she railed at him about this, he simply wrote notes to her: "Forgive me. I'm sorry."

Not about to risk the money that was coming in, she did not take up with other men. Her appointment book was filled with scrawls that said, "Depressed!"

Or, "Can't wait for trip to Bogotá!" Or, "Rick not home again. Drinking? Another woman?"

At that delicate stage in early 1988, the marriage might have foundered if, in one of the rare moments when they enjoyed intercourse, Rosario had not become pregnant. She'd already suffered one miscarriage, and the memory of that brought them both together. This time she gave birth in November to a son, who was christened Paul after the middle name of Rick's father.

As for Rick's work performance at the Rome station, it was the same old story. His managerial skills in running the "enemy targets" branch were rated consistently positive. But once again, his efforts in developing source leads—the benchmark of a successful case officer operating overseas—were desultory at best. In this regard, his last evaluation carried the comment that "his full potential had not been realized here in Rome." Rick would argue that much of the criticism leveled against him was because the Rome station chief had a personal animus against him—which was true. One of the things that drove the station chief wild was Rick's procrastination in submitting operational expense reports. What was he doing out there? Rick's reaction left everyone nonplussed. He simply ceased to report them at all. At worst, these evaluations showed that while Rick was a solid desk officer, better suited in a slot at Langley, he would never be a star in the field. It did not occur to anyone that for his true masters, he'd already achieved stardom.

In the twenty-twenty hindsight concerning Rick in Rome, there was an avalanche of reports about Rick drinking his lunch, staggering back to his office unable to function, that he had been reprimanded (verbally) for his alcohol dependency, that he had been counseled "in an almost sheepish way" by a station manager to seek help, that he was "one of the worst drunks in the outfit," which, of course, also indicated that he had plenty of competition. Not a single one of these observations, however, ever appeared in his official record. His Rome duty tour, originally ticketed for two years, was even extended for another twelve months.

In late May 1989, Rick met "Vlad" in a clandestine visit to the Soviet compound for the third and last time in Rome. Rick was scheduled to return to Langley that summer.

Rick gave up the name of a ranking officer whom he learned the agency had recruited in the KGB's Second Chief Directorate in Moscow, which was responsible for counterintelligence and state security within the borders of the Soviet Union. Through him the CIA was providing false leads about assets it was running there.

Rick had already passed word of his imminent departure from Italy. "Vlad," over vodka, continued to stroke Rick, saying how pleased Moscow was with him, how valued he was, and how his fervent friends in the KGB looked forward to an enduring productive relationship in the States. "Vlad" noted that while in Rome Rick had received nearly $900,000. And he gave Rick a balance sheet, as of May 1, 1989, showing that overall a total of two million seven hundred and five thousand dollars was appropriated for him. From the opening of Rick's account in a bank (unnamed), some $385,000 had accumulated in compounded interest. There had been an additional profit of about $15,000 realized in the bonds (again unnamed) that were purchased on his behalf. The figures were calculated down to the penny. In sum, $1,881,811.51 had been delivered to Rick. There remained at the moment $1,535,077.28 yet to be dispersed. Rick's annual salary would remain $300,000.

There was a little postscript surprise. Five Polaroid photographs showed a view through birch trees of a river. It was property that was being held for him in the USSR. Someday he could have his own dacha on it. Rick wondered if it were near Edward Lee Howard's dacha. In any event, he couldn't see himself living there—or rather, he couldn't see Rosario going along with it. He always figured, come retirement, it would be Bogotá. Still, he was touched by the gesture. Another reminder of how much these guys cared for him.

"Vlad" raised his glass, smiling warmly, as Rick dizzily absorbed what he'd been shown. "To your good health! To our comradeship!" said "Vlad" in English. And then the by now familiar, "*Na zdorovia!*"

Rick was handed a list of instructions that Moscow Center wanted followed upon his return to Langley.

Of the highest priority was a continuing flow of information about CIA penetrations into the KGB, the GRU, and the Soviet diplomatic corps.

Next were double-agent incursions. There was evidence that they were increasingly being employed by the agency now that there were signs of a breakdown in discipline in the Soviet-bloc nations and unrest in some of the republics that made up the Soviet Union.

Rick was warned as well that there also was evidence that the CIA was becoming more conscious of possible mole activity and that traps were being set, especially computer traps, that might snare someone breaking into "sensitive compartmented information" codes, an agency classification higher than top secret.

Rick previously had been informed that when he got back to Washington, diplomatic intermediaries like "Sam" and "Sam II" would no longer be utilized to pass on money. Since he now couldn't fly up to Zurich whenever he felt like it, he'd asked that wire transfers be made to the Credit Suisse account he had in his mother-in-law's name.

This, he was told, was out of the question, leaving, as it would, electronic tracks. The alternative was to employ special "cannels" [sic]. The KGB took some pains to explain what was entailed here. It meant that "illegals"—operatives not covered by diplomatic immunity—had to be employed. "We would have to open very sensitive information about your account to *some people*." And if there was a hitch—it had "unfortunately happened" in the past—"our man would have to go to the same bank for a second time [and] there could be 'questions.' " And nobody, including Rick, desired to attract undue "attention."

The bottom line was that despite all the exotic technological advances that sent money humming around the world, exchanges between Rick and the KGB would be based on tried-and-true espionage tradecraft, the use of signal sites and dead drops—and furtive meetings in faraway places.

Signal sites were markings at specific locations indicating that a pickup or lay-down was ready. Dead drops were obscure hiding places where documents or cash, in heavily taped black plastic, would be loaded or unloaded without the participants ever personally coming in contact. Rick's first-year schedule was to lay down his packaged information on the third Thursday of every third month. His first signal site, which would show that he had loaded a dead drop, was called "Hotel"—a chalk mark on a specified brick in a wall at St. Thomas the Apostle school on Woodley Road in northwest Washington. If some sort of an emergency came up, he was also to use the brick to signal this. The brick was monitored every day by KGB officers driving downtown to the embassy. Meanwhile, the dead drop, designated "Bridge," was a space beneath the far end of a pedestrian bridge over a meandering

stream in a park where Little Falls Parkway intersected with Massachusetts Avenue just outside the
D.C. line in Maryland. If the chalk mark on the brick
was gone when Rick checked it in the morning, the
pickup had been made.

For his cash, in a similar procedure on the third
Saturday of the following month, the Soviets would
use signal site "North," a telephone pole on Military
Road in Virginia not far from the CIA's Langley
headquarters. Early Sunday morning, before traffic
started, Rick would drive to dead drop "Pipe," a
culvert under a bridle path in a remote section of huge
Wheaton Regional Park, also in Maryland, to get his
money package. On the way home, he'd regularly
pull in at Dunkin' Donuts on University Boulevard in
Wheaton and while sipping coffee and nibbling on a
frosted cruller in his Jaguar, he'd count the bills.

In Rome, "Vlad" told him that under the new
dead drop system, the amounts of cash would be
necessarily smaller, averaging ten thousand dollars.
But when Rick protested, an agreement was reached
to at least double the figure.

The big hunk of his salary would be handed over
next summer at their annual meeting. This one would
be in Vienna. He'd be advised as to the exact time and
place of the rendezvous. That way, he could carry the
money himself to Zurich and deposit it directly into
the Credit Suisse account he'd set up in Cecilia's
name.

On July 25, 1989, Rick, Rosario, and infant Paul
flew from Rome to Washington. First class, of course.

A week later, on August 1, Rick contracted to buy a
home on North Randolph Street in the Country Club
Hills section of North Arlington. It was the first place
that the realtor showed him. The neighborhood did
not boast mansions. Building lots were relatively

small, the homes about twenty feet apart. But the immediate surroundings said upper middle class in capital letters. The two-story house was painted-gray brick with red shutters and had a two-car garage. Off the foyer on the left as you entered, there was a large kitchen with a spacious eating area. The kitchen needed work, but Rosario saw to the renovations—twice, as a matter of fact—to the tune of $95,000. To the right, there was a study for Rick. In the rear there was a living room more than thirty feet long that opened two steps down into a library. Best of all, there was no backyard across which neighbors could stare. Instead, the ground behind the house rose steeply at least seventy feet, and the homes above were hardly visible through the summer foliage. Rick would have a large deck constructed that featured a giant hot tub. Upstairs, there was a master bedroom, two smaller bedrooms, and a study of her own for Rosario. There was a full-size basement easily convertible to additional living space, and Rick would install a small kitchen, a bath and shower, and another bedroom. Not only Cecilia, but Rosario's younger brother, Pablo, would be frequent visitors from Colombia. There was also room for a play area for Paul that featured a puppet theater. The location was very convenient to CIA headquarters in McLean, ten minutes at most even at rush hour. Most important, Rosario liked it—and it would be in both their names.

The seller had told the realtor to ask for $540,000 and negotiate down. But Rick didn't haggle for a second. The price was fine and he'd pay in cash. The realtor gulped. My God, this guy's wife was from Colombia! Drug dealers? He had to cover himself and so made a hesitant inquiry. His wife, Rick archly informed him, was from an extremely prominent and wealthy family in her native country. Why should he go through the hassle of mortgage applications and outrageous interest payments that would end up doubling the cost of the house? The realtor didn't have any fast answers, nor did he look for one. Rick immediately wrote out a Dominion check for the full amount from funds wired in from Cecilia's Credit Suisse account. Let's see anyone make something out of that, he thought.

During Rick Ames's duty tour in Rome, the CIA's look into its compromised cases continued—but barely.

Once in a while FBI agents from headquarters would meet with the special task force the agency had set up to discuss the compromises, to ascertain if any new information, new explanations, had turned up about them. But as far as the CIA was concerned, they were arm's length affairs.

One of the FBI agents in attendance was Jim Holt, Valery Martynov's former handler. "We didn't really get involved in how they were handling their own cases," he recalled. "In that regard, we didn't play much of a role. There was a periodic exchange of information. It was handled more or less on a liaison basis. And we received reporting from time to time about operations they had that were perceived to be in trouble. . . . It tended to follow lines of individual cases more than a concerted effort to address a whole collection of them."

For Holt, it was frustrating—and personal.

"I had a lot of different feelings," he recalled in his quiet manner. "And they occurred largely on two different levels, which you had to separate. You have to remain objective, because if you don't, you tend to lose your professionalism and that's critical to maintain. But it was hard to keep out the personal side, which is one of the levels I was referring to. And that was because of my involvement with this man,

Martynov, who I grew to know fairly well and in many ways respect. We had a lot in common, families and that sort of thing. It was completely devastating to me when I learned that, number one, he was in trouble, and then, down the road, that he'd been executed.

"Right away, you start searching in your own mind about what caused this, just looking for anything, any reason you could come up with, anything that you might have done. It's just a terrible feeling to find out that somebody you knew was executed, murdered. I'd been in counterintelligence for a long time and something like this had never happened to me. So you have to compartment your feelings so it doesn't cloud your professional judgment. You have to force yourself to be even more objective professionally when you go through the process of what went wrong and how it went wrong and who was to blame, if anybody. And it isn't easy. You have known this man, Martynov. You have spent dozens of hours with him. You know, he was more than a source. He was a live human being."

Jim Holt never doubted that it had been the result of a human penetration—a murderous mole—in the agency. He tried to picture who would do what he had done. "We talked about the kind of person we were looking for. We did this with our colleagues out there [at Langley] as well as privately among ourselves. I concluded that whoever he was, he had to be a greedy, no-good, amoral stone killer, a kind of subhuman species because of the consequences of his actions, the unbelievable scope of it, causing the deaths of at least twelve people we know of. The way he did it. How can you do that?"

Then, even these meetings petered out. The agency's special task force was concentrating its energies on creating the new Counterintelligence Center that CIA director William Webster wanted. Further looks into the compromises were left to a single investigator from the agency's security office. By the end of 1988, according to the CIA inspector general's report that eventually would review all this, the investigator had scrutinized ninety employees in the Soviet/East Europe division who displayed character vulnerabilities that the KGB might have been able to exploit. He had come up with ten possible suspects. The bad news was that among them "there were so many problem personalities . . . that no one stands out." And more depressing, none of the ten could be tied to the first wave of compromises that included Martynov and Motorin.

Nonetheless the investigator plowed on, despite being first diverted by having to attend a required training program and next by a trip to Germany to examine East German intelligence files that had been opened up after the Berlin Wall came crashing down in late 1989.

By now, at Langley, Rick Ames was back in the catbird seat as Western Europe branch chief of Soviet counterintelligence, according him access to endless CIA operations that involved either Soviet or Soviet-bloc agents traveling to or residing in Western Europe. Any flicker of fear that he'd had that he might be unmasked immediately evaporated.

But it hadn't gone unnoticed that a different Rick had returned from Rome, far more polished in appearance with his capped teeth and Armani suits. And for the first time, Rick Ames got some discreet investigative attention. A tip came in from another officer in the Soviet/East Europe division that Rick, who appeared to have little money when he left for Rome, had come back notably affluent, purchasing, for example, an expensive home in North Arlington, complete with costly interior renovations and extensive landscaping, and showing up in the Langley parking lot in a $49,000 red Jaguar.

The investigator's interest perked up more when he learned that not only was the sale price of the house $540,000, but there was no record of a mortgage. Cautionary flags went up, though, when inquiries to the Rome station revealed that it was common knowledge there that Ames's wife had come into a substantial inheritance. He was the same investigator who had wasted time more than a year before chasing after a spendthrift agency officer, suspiciously living beyond his apparent means, who turned out to have married a rich spouse. And the purchase of the Jaguar didn't prove to be very exciting considering the money Rick allegedly had access to; however extravagant, he was making monthly payments on it. Some guys just loved cars.

Still, the investigator had requested that the Treasury Department look into any currency transactions Rick might have made. There were, he was told, three blips on the screen that exceeded the $10,000 limit. One was a $13,000 cash deposit, another a deposit for $15,000, and a third when Rick had exchanged lire into $22,017 after he returned from Rome. Actually, Rick made these deposits on purpose—to test the enforcement waters and, if he were called on them, to use Rosario's supposed wealth to head off any additional probing about other deposits.

More bids for Rick's financial state were made. A federal credit union check showed nothing unusual, no outstanding debt load other than $25,000 Rick still owed on the Jaguar. A cable was sent to the Bogotá station for more background on Rosario. The answer was a familiar refrain. She came from a prominent, well-established Colombian family. This time there was an added fillip. Rosario's relatives were into real estate and various commercial enterprises, including a flourishing export/import trade, and were said to have charitably donated land worth millions for a soccer field and sports arena for the city's impoverished. Where the Bogotá station got this information from was never nailed down. The original request was not high priority, and in a subsequent review, it seemed that the station had what were considered to be far more urgent matters to contend with.

None of these anomalies were conveyed to the FBI. Even in the CIA, they remained tightly held within the operations directorate. The expertise of the agency's financial management office was not solicited, nor was that of the inspector general's auditors. The feeling was that persons outside the directorate just weren't attuned to its culture, to the sensitivity of the situation.

Only one officer in the directorate was outspokenly after Rick. He was Paul Redmond, a stocky, gruff man who spiced his language with obscenities. He'd been a branch chief with Rick in the Soviet/East Europe division, had initially headed up the Yurchenko task force, was on the special four-man task force looking futilely into the compromises, and now was deputy chief of the Counterintelligence Center. For him, Rick had always been a fuck-up and maybe a lot worse. But Redmond's known distaste for Rick colored the attitude of others. Simply because you disliked someone didn't automatically make him a traitor. And the KGB was still hard at work covering for Rick. Word was received from an alleged KGB defector that a CIA case officer, otherwise unidentified, had been recruited in Moscow in the mid-1970s. Almost a year was spent trying to match this up with a current or former employee—to no avail.

Most bothersome of all—and the investigator never could forget it—was that Rick was making no attempt to disguise his affluence. That simply didn't fit a mole's MO. About the only thing left was to give him a polygraph. And even this was circled with great wariness. His last polygraph had been in 1986 before he went to Rome. The normal cycle for polygraphs was every five years. He wasn't due for another one until 1991. Suppose something was there, the argument went. Why alert him unnecessarily?

The polygraph examination was a joke.

It took place on April 12, 1991. When the FBI gave a polygraph, a certain psychological ambiance was created. A little apprehension on the subject's part was desired. Anything being hidden? This was not going to be all fun and games. But with Rick, as far as the agency polygrapher was concerned, it was another routine examination to get over with. He had not been provided with any background on why it was being given, other than that there should be some questions about Rick's finances.

Rick had prepped himself for precisely that, fully expecting to be queried especially about the Arlington house. Along with his dead drop cash pickups, he'd been to Vienna the previous summer, where "Vlad" had handed over $150,000 that he'd put in Cecilia's account as her trustee. And he was preparing to go to Bogotá in a few months to receive another $150,000. So even before the polygraph started, to help himself relax, he was chatting it up with the examiner, volunteering how lucky he was to have a wealthy mother-in-law, that as a result of her largesse, he'd acquired property in Colombia and was reaping the profits of some small but lucrative investments.

During the examination itself, asked only a standard question about whether he was experiencing any financial difficulties, Rick confidently replied, "No," elaborating again, as though he'd come to believe it himself, about good old Cecilia's money and the doors it had opened for him. He made it seem as if he were staying in the CIA, where he was earning slightly under seventy thousand dollars, as a patriotic gesture.

His sole sign of deception was when he was asked if he had concealed any contacts with foreign nationals. Rick explained that this might be because of his sometimes sloppy note keeping. More than once he had been called on the carpet for it. In Rome, he said, he'd been meeting with a Soviet diplomat he hoped to recruit and may have overlooked a couple of encounters. The more he thought about it, he added, the more the possibility of this upset him.

As was standard, the polygrapher called it a day and marked the examination "incomplete." As was also standard, Rick was invited to return for a second go-round. A different polygrapher was present to administer the test. Since it was no longer an issue, he did not repeat any questions relating to personal finances. And this time, as to the nonreporting of foreign contacts, Rick breezed right through. Upon reconsideration, he said, there weren't any.

On the record, he had passed. If Rick Ames was a Soviet spy, there certainly wasn't any proof of it. To borrow a favorite CIA word, he had created a pretty good "legend" for himself.

The old compromises, however, wouldn't go away. And new CIA operations were running into deep trouble. Something was still alive, well, and bad. Most electrifying—and humiliating—was the news that GRU general Dimitr Polyakov, the FBI's fabled "Top Hat," the CIA's self-proclaimed crown jewel source it had code-named "Accord," now lay dead in an unmarked grave. As if to underscore the hard times that the CIA's Soviet intelligence apparatus had fallen on, the agency learned about it like everyone else—in the pages of the Moscow newspaper *Pravda* some two years after the fact. Polyakov had been executed on March 15, 1988.

The CIA was out of options. In the spring of 1991 the agency's Paul Redmond finally was permitted to come to the FBI and say, "We have blood on our hands," that the agency needed help. At long last, a joint no-holds-barred investigation with the FBI would commence into what was clearly an ongoing cancer of the most pernicious kind—one that had to be excised no matter what it took or how much time was required.

7

Playactor, the FBI's code name for the investigation, was dreamed up by agent Jim Milburn. Together with Jim Holt, Milburn was assigned by headquarters to begin working with analysts at Langley.

Without knowing anything about Rick Ames or his youthful theatrical ambitions, Milburn had always felt that the person being sought had to be someone who was in fact a consummate actor, who could play a role and deceive everybody around him for a very long time and not crumble under the weight of what he was doing or the guilt of it—someone for whom this was perhaps the role of a lifetime.

Later, after it was all over, Milburn would say, "It was drama beyond Rick's wildest dreams. And acting was the one thing he had the utmost confidence in. He felt he had real worth as an actor and was unfairly denied his chance for a career on the stage."

Milburn recalled that when Rick was driving out to Andrews Air Force Base to meet the defecting Vitaly Yurchenko, knowing that Yurchenko once had been a senior officer in Directorate K, the KGB's foreign counterintelligence wing, you'd think he'd have been shaking in his boots that Yurchenko would step off the plane and say, "The spy you are looking for is Aldrich Ames."

"But when we asked Rick about this," Milburn said, "he said he didn't really prepare himself for anything of the sort. I truly believe that this was so. The worst he expected was that Yurchenko might have heard talk about an active mole, which was why he wrote that note in Russian about whether there was something special Yurchenko wanted to say to somebody at the top. We asked Rick, 'What would you have done when you got in that car with Yurchenko if he had described you—maybe not have given your name—but described you to a tee?' And he said, 'I would have had to work my way out of it. I would have had to talk my way out of it. I would have done whatever I had to do.' And I don't think Rick doubted for a minute that he couldn't have improvised and pulled it off. It was what he gloried in. Except for a couple of bad moments he had in Rome that he got over, I think it thrilled him every time he did a dead drop or had a clandestine meeting. Rick always refused to admit he got a kick out of it, but then he'd make a point of insisting that the pressure never bothered him in the slightest. So he really was telling us in a negative way that he kind of enjoyed it."

At the time Playactor got under way, Milburn was supervising a headquarters Soviet analytical group. A reticent man with receding reddish hair, he had an unusual background for the counterintelligence agent that he'd been for the past fifteen years. He had come out of tiny Thiel College in western Pennsylvania, a sociology and psychology major. He was working with kids in a juvenile detention center when he heard about an opening in the bureau's personnel office. After he had been there two years, the FBI, intent on buttressing its sophistication in foreign counterintelligence, started scouting around for analysts. Jim Milburn jumped right in. He'd always been fascinated by what made people tick in general, and from then on he immersed himself in what made the KGB tick in particular. It became axiomatic for CI squad agents in the Washington Field Office to seek out Milburn for some esoteric bit of information about the KGB—*if* they could find him, buried as he most often was in an office outside headquarters, poring over KGB arcana, trying to figure out what its various directorates were up to, looking for patterns, how the KGB's First Chief Directorate for worldwide intelligence was operating, how it was trying to recruit sources, what new gimmicks were being employed.

And like Jim Holt, Milburn had a personal stake in Playactor, maybe not quite as personal, but still it counted for something. When CI squad agent Mike Morton had first recruited Major Sergei Motorin in the early 1980s, Motorin insisted that he would work only with Morton, period, or no deal. This went against all the rules. A recruiter recruited, a handler handled. But Milburn, recognizing the special rapport the two enjoyed, fully supported the arrangement. Still, it was tough for Morton to do it alone, trying to remember what questions to ask, what follow-ups to pursue, and all the while trying to keep the skittish Motorin reassured, emotionally together, making sure that the fragile bonds that had brought them together in the first place were not snapped. So Milburn had met with Mike Morton constantly to review what had been done, what was next on the agenda, guiding and advising him. Although Milburn never actually met the KGB major, he felt that he had come to know him quite well. And then, of course, he learned that Motorin had not just been shot, which was bad enough, but that he'd been tortured to death.

Milburn and Holt began their work with two senior female analysts at Langley in July 1991. They were housed in the Counterintelligence Center on the ground floor of the gleaming glass-and-steel addition to the original concrete fortresslike CIA facility.

They were not at all hidden from view. You had to know a special lock combination to enter the center proper, but once inside, most of the space was open, given over to partitioned workstations, much like what might be found in a stock brokerage firm, a large insurance company, or a newspaper city room. Milburn, Holt, and one of the CIA analysts were in adjoining cubicles in a rear corner that overlooked an employee parking lot. If privacy for discussions was needed, there was a conference room available—in fact, the agency seemed to have no lack of conference rooms—or, as usually happened, everyone huddled in the closed office of the senior analyst for Skylight (the CIA's code name for the investigation), a middle-aged woman of considerable prestige named Jean Vertefeuille.

The appearance of FBI agents like Holt and Milburn by itself would not cause much notice. Both of them, Milburn especially, were familiar sights. On the other hand, unwanted gossip—to say nothing of putting their quarry on alert—might be provoked by the fact that they weren't dropping by for a one- or two-day visit but were going to be around for a prolonged period, using agency computers, scrutinizing endless files. So the "legend"—their cover—was that the old 1985 compromises were being reviewed again. It was hardly a man-bites-dog story. Something like this had been going on in fits and starts for as long as anyone in the operations directorate could remember.

Holt and Milburn were astonished by the number of agency case compromises as well as major operations—thirty of them. Since the CIA was mandated by law to gather positive intelligence, it had to be informed sooner or later of all the sources the FBI had developed. But it didn't work the other way around. The FBI remained in the dark about what the CIA was doing, notably the details of what had gone wrong. Until now.

Most of the compromises involved the Soviets. So the logical place to start, where the damage most likely had occurred, was in the division where Rick, except for his Rome interlude, had been a counterintelligence branch chief. That put Rick Ames on the list of names that was being compiled. At the top of it, as a matter of fact. But only alphabetically.

Even narrowing the focus to the Soviet/East Europe division presented a daunting task. There were two hundred CIA officers in the division. Short of a miraculous breakthrough, months of work lay ahead. No one doubted that a human penetration had taken place. Was there more than one needle in the haystack, however? Perhaps there wasn't one person against whom all the compromises could be attributed. Perhaps one person was responsible for a number of them and someone else the rest. Right then, though, neither Jim Holt nor Jim Milburn wanted to think about something like that happening.

"The approach," Holt recalled, "was to go through the cases or operations that were believed to be compromised, to look at each one separately to determine if there were any smoking guns or patently obvious reasons for them. And then to look at the group collectively—this universe of two hundred people we had—and to see literally who among them had access to the operations and what role they played. Some access, of course, was broader or more critical than others. We also had to look at factors beyond this that might help us—the information that the agency's special task force had been picking up over the last

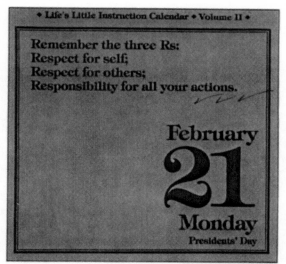

◆ Life's Little Instruction Calendar ◆ Volume II ◆

Remember the three Rs:
Respect for self;
Respect for others;
Responsibility for all your actions.

February

21

Monday

Presidents' Day

A page from a desk calendar found in Ames's
home on the day of his arrest.

Valery Martynov (*left*) and Sergei Motorin, Ames's
first two victims.

Sergei Chuvakhin, one of Ames's first important
contacts with the KGB.

A NEW DD

To provide a continuity of our exchange we propose a new DD instead of "Creek"

The name of a new DD ----- "GRound"

DD location. The foot bridge over the creek in "Rock Creek", located two yards North-West from the T-type junction of Pinehurst pkwy and Beach dr (ADC "ashington DC street map, p.3, F-7 or Montgomer; Co MD, p.39, C-5).

Package site. Under the bridge corner nearest to the junction (South-East corner).

Permanent signal location. The bridge over Rock creek now Massachusetts ave (ADC street map "ashington DC & vicinity p.9, F-9) Metallic fence of the bridge turn into low wooden one.

Type of signal ----- the horizontal line by black lead - is to be put on the wooden post of the low fence, nearest to the intersection of Massachusetts ave with Whitehaven st.
The name of this signal is "Hill".

Your actions with DD "GRound".

Till 3.00 any working day You mark signal "Hill". The appearance of it means that at the same day till 19.00 You load "Ground". You may load "Ground" and mark "Hill" a day before (first street).

We shall check "Hill" every working day from 3.00 to 9.00. If we see "Hill", we shall unload "Ground" from 19.00 to 22.00 and then erase Your mark at "Hill". If Your mark at "Hill" is still by 23.00 it means that we did not unload "Ground" and You ought to returne to "Ground" that evening or early next morning to retrieve Your package. You could repeat this operation any suitable for You working day.

"y these DDs we hope to receive Your disks with info, Your proposals on alternate dates and places of personal mtgs in Bogota or anywhere.

We propose that You check DD "GRound" and "Hill" signal on place you give only after that us Your agreement or disagreement with it by "Bridge" during our next exchange in march or April 1992.
We ask You not to use "Ground" before giving us Your opinion about a safety of it. We shall wait for Your replay. IN 3.00 ....
OF MARCH 1992

Instructions from the Russians to Ames on how to make one of his "dead drops."

One of the various drop sites in and around Washington, D.C. This one—a culvert—is in Wheaton Regional Park in Maryland.

Mailbox with chalk mark visible on side, which signaled Ames's intent to go to Bogotá to meet with his Russian handler.

The FBI's Robert "Bear" Bryant, who was in charge of the bureau's pursuit of Ames.

Les Wiser Jr. of the FBI, who put his career on the line when tracking down Ames.

FBI director Louis Freeh, who decided the time had come to arrest Ames.

I AM READY TO MEET
AT B ON 1 OCT.
        I CANNOT READ
NORTH 13 - 19 SEPT.
        IF YOU WILL
MEET AT B ON 1 OCT.
PLS SIGNAL NORTH 4
OF 20 SEPT TO CONFI.
NO MESSAGE AT PIPE.
        IF YOU CANNOT MEE.
1 OCT, SIGNAL NORTH AFTER
27 SEPT WITH MESSAGE AT
    PIPE.

The yellow Post-it, found in Ames's garbage, the first direct evidence that he was spying for Moscow.

The actual moment of Ames's arrest.

```
              Dear Friend,
this is Your balance sheet as on the day 1, 1989.

   * All in all You have been appropriated ----  2,705,000 $
   * From the time of oppening of Your
     account in our Bank (December 26,
     1986) Your profit is --------------------  385,077$ 28c
   (including  14,468$ 94c as profit on bonds, which we
   bought for You on the sum of  250,000$)
   * Since December 1986 Your salary is ------  300,000$
   * All in all we have delivered to You -----  1,881,811$ 51c
   * On the above date You have on Your
     account (including 250,000$ in bonds) --- 1,535,077$ 28c

    P.S.  We believe that these pictures would give You some
idea about the beautiful piece of land on the river bank,
which from now belongs to You forever. We decided not to take
pictures of housing in this area with the understanding that
You have much better idea of how Your country house (dacha)
should look like.

    Good luck.
```

An accounting statement of monies paid
to Ames by the Russians, as of 1989.

```
    My dear friends:

        I write this in some haste on Tues evening, 1 September. I
am afraid that the signal HILL is not well-thought-out;
the wooden post is often damp and mildewed -- discolored --
and the pencil mark I made on the morning of 19 August does not
appear to have been observed.  After making the signal at HILL with
pencil at about 0700 on 19 August, I placed the drop at GROUND
about 1600 that same day. I was worried about the visibility of
the signal and waited until daylight of 20 August to check to see
if it had been erased -- it did not appear to have been erased,
and I retrieved my package (which included documents!) later that
day. Unfortunately, I left Washington for a vacation trip
to California on 21 August, returning on 30 August. I will signal
HILL on Weds morning, 2 September, but this time using chalk
instead of pencil. If my package is not retrieved during the
evening of 2 September, I will return to the old, SMILE, signal
site to mark it on 4 September and put my package down
that afternoon. In any case, I'll keep trying until you get it.
Given the shortness of time before our next meeting, I am putting
a note on the package which I hope will cause the people here to
send you a telegram confirming my intent to make our scheduled
meeting on 5/6 October. Best regards, K|
```

Ames complaining about a signal site on
Massachusetts Avenue.

Rosario Ames getting into her
Honda.

FBI mug shots of Rick and Rosario Ames.

few years, its efforts to get to the bottom of things, which had been unavailable to us, as well as our own past studies in light of what we were now learning.''

It was, said Holt with some understatement, ''quite a bit of data to look at initially. You tried to establish links, identify points of vulnerability, poor tradecraft, or maybe a source got cold feet and went off into the sunset. You know, you're meeting a source regularly and suddenly he doesn't show up. Was it something innocuous, like a true illness in his family, or was he done in? You would look to see how communications were handled, contacts made, how long they had gone on, and what the circumstances were when they ceased. Was the compromised case called back to Russia? Did he begin to indicate signs of nervousness?''

And there was access—*and* access. In the strictest sense, the most narrow interpretation, it was defined as the legitimate need-to-know authority or duty to actually read a particular file, to know about a case, be directly involved, or have some official connection with an operation. The real name of the source being run might not be known, but if the circumstances surrounding him could be passed on to the KGB in sufficient detail, that was all it would take.

The other, unofficial access, could be just as malevolent. It hinged on the personality of someone in the agency. Was he always strolling about, a corridor talker, a cigarette-break gossiper, someone who'd let something slip to a carpool buddy?

Week after week, Holt, Milburn, and two CIA analysts independently studied the dossiers of all two hundred division officers, as well as those of ten additional high-level CIA executives outside the division whose command positions might have enabled them to obtain specific knowledge about cases that were compromised. "It got to be a little touchy at times," Holt remembered.

Reading many of these personnel records was largely unsatisfactory—for the most part they were written in conservative bureaucratese, portraying essentially apple-pie citizens, born-and-bred American Chevrolet owners, patriots in the intelligence community who'd sacrificed much to serve the U.S. government, and certainly not reflecting the amorality, the evil, that Holt envisioned and was searching for.

"We have to find the answer," Holt told Milburn riding back from Langley one afternoon. "How could this son of a bitch year after year deliberately pass on information he knows is going to destroy lives?"

"Yeah," Milburn said. "It's unbelievable. It's like nothing we've ever seen."

Still, hints of emotional upset surfaced that the Soviets might have capitalized on one way or another. A messy divorce. A gravely sick family member. Financial problems.

For Holt and Milburn, they were all simply names. Jean Vertefeuille and the second CIA analyst, Sandy Grimes, knew them personally. Especially Vertefeuille. At first, the two FBI agents were chary about this, that it might color objective judgment. But it soon became apparent that their CIA counterparts were as determined as they were to get to the bottom of this and would provide invaluable, time-saving insights.

"What about this guy?" Milburn said. "Look at these two polygraphs. In the first one, he said that the KGB pitched him and he turned them down, even reported it when it happened. But it says here the polygrapher wasn't completely satisfied with the response. So he was moved to a less sensitive job. And then he takes another poly five years later, and there's another flutter."

"First of all," Vertefeuille said, "we all know that

polygraphs can be unreliable, and it's especially true for this fellow. I know him well. He's a reactor. High-strung, nervous. If you walk up behind him and say 'Boo!' he'll jump six feet in the air. We just don't think he's that big a concern. He couldn't possibly be our man."

In Vertefeuille's office, Jim Holt pointed to the comments in another officer's evaluation sheet. "What's this mean," Holt asked, "when it says that he needs more counseling in his communications methods?"

Oh, said Vertefeuille, she knew about him as well. "They were just trying to be nice. What they really meant was that he was ineffective, useless. They were covering up his deficiencies. I can't defend the practice, but that's the way it is sometimes."

For still other officers, either Vertefeuille or Grimes would say, "You're right, it looks bad, but he's not as bad as it looks on paper." Or, "We agree this is someone who ought to have been gotten rid of a long time ago, but the fact is that he just didn't have the right access."

Holt and Milburn would often play devil's advocate, but in almost every instance, upon further review, the two CIA analysts turned out to be right. By late fall, after the initial go-round, about half of the original two hundred agency employees had been eliminated. The determining factor was an indisputable lack of access to the compromised cases.

In the midst of all this, what first appeared to be the miraculous breakthrough arrived at Playactor's doorstep. Word of the investigation being conducted at Langley had spread over the grapevine, and a case officer at the Bonn station reported that a KGB source he claimed to be developing was saying that the Soviets had in fact penetrated the agency's secret West Virginia communications center, an old allegation the

FBI did not know about. The mole, Russian born, was said to be still active. But when the case officer was recalled for further questioning, it became quickly evident that he'd cooked up the whole thing to advance his career, and he was fired.

A decision was made to interview those still on the list.

The interviews were purposely designed to be non-confrontational, just a fact-finding mission. The idea was not to indicate that any of those being called in were under suspicion.

Jean Vertefeuille would usually take the lead. "Come in and have a seat," she'd say. "As you may or may not know, we're still looking at the compromises that occurred in 1985 in our Soviet operations. And once again, as you probably know, Edward Lee Howard and perhaps a couple of other factors may. have contributed to some of them. But we want to take one last step, make one last attempt, to see if we can tie down all those things. So we'd like to ask you today to run through some of your thoughts on that, and would you start by refreshing us— Oh, by the way, these are our colleagues from the FBI, who are working with us on this."

Holt and Milburn were introduced. And then Vertefeuille said, "Why don't we get started and you tell us where you were in 1985?"

And the questions, delivered in a conspiratorial don't-be-concerned, this-is-between-us manner, followed:

"Can you remember what were you doing at that time?"

"Who were you working for? Was there any change in your supervisors? Did that affect you in any way?"

"How did the paper flow in your office go?"

"Were there changes in your responsibilities? Were

you asked by anyone to do anything out of the ordinary? And if so, by whom?"

Those being interviewed were encouraged to talk about their co-workers:
"Was there anybody you worked with who seemed unduly curious about operations he shouldn't have had an interest in?"
"Can you think of anybody you worked with during that time period who troubled you?"

Their advice and counsel would be elicited:
"What do you personally think happened?"
"Why do you think these cases were compromised?"
"Do you think it was a mole?"
"Do you think it was a collection of cases that fell individually on their own merit, or lack thereof?"
"Could there have been screw-ups in tradecraft?"
"Tell us, please. What are your thoughts?"

The hope was to obtain some insights that weren't reflected in official records.
The responses varied wildly.
One employee said, "Well, it always looked bad to me. Maybe I've been reading too many thrillers, but I always thought it was a mole."
Another said, "It's probably something technical. It's in our communications. It has to be."
Animosities surfaced. So-and-so had been constantly "nosy." So-and-so was a boozer. So-and-so was a wife beater, and he was going through a "bad divorce when one or two of these things happened."
Rick Ames was singled out in three of the interviews. "He was real slovenly," was one characterization. "Jesus, you ought to have smelled his breath. Then he goes off to Rome and comes back and buys

this big house and car and is wearing thousand-dollar suits. Where the hell is he getting all the money?''

Rick himself was interviewed. After his return from Rome, he'd served for three months as Western Europe branch chief in his old division. In a divisional reorganization, he was next appointed operational chief of the Czechoslovakia branch and was on a promotion board for midlevel operational officers. This enabled him to obtain all their identities and personnel records, which he promptly placed in dead drop "Bridge" for a KGB pickup. When the Communist regime disintegrated in Czechoslovakia in 1990, Rick started lobbying for a more challenging post. Among those he had in mind was deputy chief of the Moscow station. It would be, he said, "a fitting finale" to his career. Around then, he also flew to Vienna for his rendezvous with "Vlad" and another $150,000.

At the time of his interview, Rick had just come off being part of an analysis group in the Counterintelligence Center and was back in the Soviet/East Europe division heading up a KGB study team, again privy to a wide range of division records.

He was, Jim Holt remembered, very cool, relaxed, apparently anxious to be helpful, even volunteering that more than once he had been lax about not locking up classified documents in his safe, as if chagrined at the thought that some unknown person might have rifled through them. That, he explained, had been at an especially difficult time in his life, when he'd been distracted by a drawn-out divorce proceeding. He had since made a point of ensuring that this wasn't repeated. He also acknowledged quite forwardly that he was familiar with several of the compromised cases. In his counterintelligence slot, how could he not be?

He was asked specifically about Sergei Motorin, code-named "Gauze." Rick seemed to search his memory. His response was nebulous. "I really can't recall that one," he said. "Was he operational for us?" Which, of course, Motorin wasn't.

"Get a little hypothetical with us," Jean Vertefeuille said. "If you were going to do this, if you were going to cooperate with the Soviets, how would you go about it? And would you do it more than once?"

"That's a tough one," replied Rick. "I just can't imagine myself doing something like that. But now that you ask, if I did, I probably would do it abroad. Otherwise," he mildly observed, "it'd just be too risky, don't you think?"

"Rick," Jim Holt recalled, "walked away from that interview without the slightest notion that he was any more of a concern to us than anybody else. In fact, we told him, as we told all the others, that we were talking to as many individuals as we could who had familiarity with these cases."

Still, enough questions had been raised to move Rick finally out of the Soviet/East Europe division. At the end of the year, he was assigned to the CIA's Counternarcotics Center, created in response to charges that the agency wasn't doing all it could against international drug trafficking. In fact, this did little to keep Rick from regularly dropping by his SE division to ascertain what was going on. Or forage around on his agency computer.

By early 1992, the list been narrowed down to twenty-nine suspects. And Rick, of course, was still on it. It was called the "bigot" list. It was an agency word that the FBI had adopted, but nobody in either the CIA or the bureau seemed to know where it came from. Jim Milburn was willing to settle for the obvious—someone who had the potential to be a "bad news" person.

Everyone on it had one thing in common—access. Each underwent renewed, intense scrutiny. Job performance. Sexual proclivities out of the norm. Substance abuse. Family life. Polygraph deceptiveness relating to counterintelligence issues. Even time and attendance cards at Langley were carefully perused. Who was where—in or out of the country—when compromises took place? What about unexplained income?

Of the twenty-nine, Rick was singular in his display of money. For the first time, Holt and Milburn learned about a Counterintelligence Center memo, dated December 5, 1990, requesting the security office to "open a reinvestigation of Aldrich H. Ames" based on his "lavish spending habits during the past five years." The memo conceded that "there may be a logical explanation," that the money might have come from insurance left by his late mother, but "unfortunately, we do not know the location of his mother's last residence." Another possibility was that "the money could also have come from his in-laws." The memo concluded, "There is a degree of urgency involved in our request. Since Ames has been assigned to CIC [the Counterintelligence Center], his access has been limited to a degree. Unfortunately, we are quickly running out of things for him to do without granting him greater access. It is our hope to at least get Ames through a polygraph before we are forced to take such action."

Other records showed that an agency security office investigator subsequently determined that Rick's mother had no insurance to speak of. He had checked with a federal credit union about Rick's debt status and found nothing awry. Inquiries had been made about the purported wealth of his wife's family in Colombia, and these appeared to have been corroborated by the Bogotá station. There was confirmation that Rick had made three cash bank deposits that exceeded the $10,000 limit and that the cost of his

North Arlington home was indeed $540,000, which
he'd met by whipping out a check on the spot from
funds that he told the realtor had come from his
wife's inheritance.

Still, for investigative agents like Holt and Milburn,
there were unresolved issues. When you got down to
it, this alleged Colombian money was all anecdotal.
Another cable was sent to the Bogotá station asking
for more detailed data about Rosario's family. When
did this inheritance happen? Clearly, based on Rick's
known lifestyle, it wasn't available at the time he'd
married his second wife. What about additional cash
deposits Rick might have made that did not contravene
currency transaction regulations? In checking into
Rick's financial condition, the security office investigator had limited himself to the Northwest Federal
Credit Union, apparently unaware that under existing
law the agency could probe into an employee's banking records. In his credit inquiry, though, he did
learn that Rick had two checking accounts at the
Dominion bank.

In May 1992, a fifth member was added to the
Playactor team at Langley, an agency auditor named
Dan Payne. He dispatched national security letters to
both banks and all major national credit card companies to find out the extent of Rick's—and Rosario's—
financial activity.

As it happened, at that very moment, Rick also
was as interested—and concerned—about his finances. During the first five months of the year, Rosario had run up nearly $50,000 in national credit card
bills alone, to say nothing of local retail charge accounts, outlays for her tuition at Georgetown University, where she was pursuing graduate studies, more
renovations in the house, a nanny for their son, two
alternating maids, a gardener, and, to be fair, a $25,000

down payment for a new 1992 Jaguar that he'd bought
for himself.

In a testy note to the KGB, Rick complained of his
immediate cash needs, describing it as "a very tight
and unpleasant situation." He had to sell a Swiss
certificate of deposit, he wrote, and cash in some
investments as well. He was in an untenable position.
He felt that dead drop "Pipe"—the bridal-path culvert
in Wheaton Regional Park—was certainly large
enough to "accomodate" [*sic*] $100,000.

Instantly, Rick received $30,000, another $20,000
in August.

Four months before, in February, in two locked rooms
at the Washington Field Office, now vacated by the
Pan Am 103 investigators, Tim Caruso, who had led
the 1986 Anlace investigation into the disappearance
of Valery Martynov and Sergei Motorin, finally assembled the agents he wanted for the second part of
Playactor. He had brought them in from as far away
as Georgia and Texas. The qualities he'd been looking
for included major-case experience in counterintelligence and what he called "ordinary, junkyard dogs"
who would never give up the hunt.

Like Caruso, one of the agents had made a significant career sacrifice to join Playactor. He was Mike
Anderson, then acting supervisor for the field office's
squad CI-4, which covered the most ominous of the
KGB lines operating in Washington, the line for Moscow Center's Directorate K that almost surely was
running the mole, whoever he was. But Anderson
didn't think twice about stepping down from being a
boss. He wore an FBI "Martyr's Pin." As a thirteen-
year-old kid, he never forgot the day it arrived in a
little mahogany box along with a medal that had a blue
satin ribbon. It was in memory of his dad. His father
was the resident agent in Harrisburg, Pennsylvania,

when he was killed in the line of duty. A crazed "mountain man," as he was known locally, had kidnapped a young schoolgirl, dragging her off into rugged, mountainous, heavily wooded terrain whose every nook and cranny was home to him. In the manhunt that followed, Anderson's dad was hard on his trail when he was suddenly bushwhacked. He died instantly from a shotgun blast.

And what Mike Anderson also never forgot was how FBI agents up and down the East Coast poured in on their own to help apprehend his father's killer. So, for him, taking a secondary position if his expertise was needed wasn't such a big deal. Besides, Caruso had confided, this could be the case of a lifetime for a counterintelligence agent.

Under Caruso's lead, Anderson's assignment was to go back in time. "I was detailed," he recalled, "to review old espionage cases and see if we could come up with anything new. It was just a matter of talking to the right people and seeing if all the leads we'd had were covered. We had this big wall chart that showed compromised cases where there appeared to have been a problem. Then there was [Edward Lee] Howard and other compromises that Howard didn't have access to, and we were trying to explain them. . . .

"Some leads out there said there was a problem in the Moscow station back in nineteen seventy-five. That was from more than one source. We had this Moscow penetration and we were trying to see if maybe that's going to lead us to something that's not Howard. There were five or six other cases that just needed to be wrapped up, put a nice bow on them if we could, and get rid of the background noise [multiple source information]. There was always background noise that something was there. We had to set this stuff aside once and for all and focus on, well, okay,

it's not the '75 transmits, it's not there, so maybe the
problem started here.''

The chart Tim Caruso had drawn up covered an
entire wall filled with cross-indexed squares. Across
the top were all the known compromises. There was a
dateline for them that began in 1955. Color-coded
leads were at the bottom. The different colors depicted
which sources they had come from. Manpower in the
field office CI squads was limited. Sometimes what
seemed to be a minor incident would still be pending
because of a major investigation that had come along.
Without exception, they now went on the chart and
were revisited. In the center of the chart, also color
coded, were not only the details of past FBI operations, but all the details of CIA operations that were
kept from the FBI until Jim Holt and Jim Milburn took
up residence at Langley. Looking at the chart, you
saw the entire history of compromises, suspected or
real, the seismic moments, where the hot spots were
in both time and place.

Caruso insisted that his Playactor team remain
independent of what was going on at Langley until the
right time arrived for a merging of information. Langley was going after internal leads. At the field office,
the thrust was external, reaching out, targeting potential sources, identifying them position by position,
combing names in the bureau's counterintelligence
files for someone who might volunteer, someone in
the know who could be recruited for a lot of help or
who could provide even a tiny clue.

The time couldn't have been more propitious. The
Soviet-bloc intelligence services, as once constituted,
were shattered. And by now, the old KGB itself was
in total disarray. Its leadership had erred grievously in
supporting the failed coup against Mikhail Gorbachev
in late August 1991. Gorbachev had already begun
dismantling the directorates before he was replaced by

Boris Yeltsin, who finished the job. Yeltsin created two new entities with a new set of initials—the SVRR, which would continue the overseas intelligence of the KGB's First Chief Directorate, and the MBRF, roughly the equivalent of the FBI. CI squads were picking up word all over the place about the resentment created by the purges, laments that the KGB's best men were being lost, how they were being tossed out in the most callous fashion.

Nor did Caruso want suspected moles from the Langley part of Playactor coming over in dribs and drabs, fearing a person-of-the-week syndrome that would disrupt the disciplined approach he had set up. And not until the list Holt, Milburn, and the others put together had been whittled to twenty-nine did he start accepting names that could be correlated with his own investigation.

At Langley, in August of 1992, the CIA auditor Dan Payne finally received the information he had asked for about Rick's banking and credit card activity.

The news was stunning. There were scores of cash deposits, all under ten thousand dollars, totaling more than a million dollars. The first one, for nine thousand dollars, had been on May 18, 1985. There was at least one major wire transfer to Rick via a New York bank from Credit Suisse. And his credit card payments were currently running ten to twelve thousand dollars a month.

As Rick became more and more in focus for the Langley team, his reported contacts in 1985 and 1986 with the Soviet diplomat Sergei Chuvakhin were unearthed. And the fact that he apparently had not reported many of them. The cable that had been sent to Rick in Rome requesting that he complete the reports—the one he had ignored—was found.

This was all forwarded to Playactor at the Washing-

ton Field Office. In his meetings with Chuvakhin, Rick
used the pseudonym "Richard Wells." In the reels of
stored video- and audiotapes, any contacts with Soviet
embassy personnel were keyed numerically. Rick was
Sub-375. When the reels were pulled and spun, they
automatically stopped at that number. Whether Chuvakhin's name was mentioned on the tapes didn't
matter. Support staff who monitored the phone calls
could identify a Soviet by his voice alone. A compari-
son was made of all Rick's meetings with Chuvakhin,
reported or not, and his cash deposits. They matched.

For the twenty-nine names still on the list, time
frames were established for when they were out of the
office on sick leave, annual leave, even for unexplained portions of any given day. At Langley, it was
learned that Rick had taken off for several days early
in October 1992, advising the CIA that he was going
to Bogotá to visit his mother-in-law.

One of Caruso's agents, Dell Spry, was dispatched
to the headquarters of American Airlines in Dallas/Ft.
Worth to confirm Rick's travel. Spry discovered that
Rick had in fact left Washington for Bogotá on October
2 via Miami. But he also discovered something else—
something that Rick had not reported. Airline records
showed that the day after arriving in Bogotá, he had
left for Caracas, Venezuela, where he spent three days
before returning to the United States.

He had gone there, as it turned out, for his annual
meeting with his handler. Despite all the upheavals of
the KGB in Moscow and its replacement by the
SVRR, Rick had continued to fill his dead drops and
to pick up his packets of money. Only this time, in
Caracas, "Vlad" was no longer his handler. He didn't
ask what had happened to "Vlad." His new handler
identified himself as "Andrei."

He gave Rick $150,000. "Andrei" told him that for
the coming year he would continue to receive his cash

in Washington at the dead drop "Pipe," the culvert under the bridle path in Wheaton Regional Park. To pass documents and messages, however, Rick had new signal sites. One was "Rose," a mailbox at the corner of Garfield Road and Garfield Terrace not far from the residence of Vice President Gore. Its dead drop, code-named "Ground," was a crevice under a pedestrian bridge in Rock Creek Park on the line between the District of Columbia and Montgomery County in Maryland. A second mailbox, "Smile," was at the intersection of 37th and R Streets right above Georgetown. The dead drop for it remained the crevice beneath the other walkway bridge under Little Falls Parkway and Massachusetts Avenue.

Rick also got a stern rebuke from "Andrei." The last time he'd signaled that he was about to make a drop, he'd neglected to bring chalk. Rick had run into a notions store, but it had only had crayons in stock and he'd used a white one. It had taken more than half an hour to erase the signal. "Do not repeat," his new handler warned.

By December 1992, Bear Bryant had seen enough— the unreported meetings with Chuvakhin, the correlation of these meetings with the cash deposits, the sheer number of the deposits, the access to the compromised cases, the unreported overseas travel. Bryant had grown increasingly impatient with the pace of Playactor. He wanted to open an official investigation immediately. This Ames was the guy.

But the CIA resisted furiously. Bryant just didn't understand the seriousness, the delicacy, of what was at stake. This concerned a career agency operations officer. Something like this was without parallel. You had to be absolutely certain. Besides, suppose it wasn't Ames after all. Suppose it wound up being one of the others on the bigot list. Would he not be alerted and escape? You couldn't keep an official investigation that secret. And granted, apprehending the mole was important. But just as important, *more* important, was finding out how he had operated, whom he had been in contact with, what secrets he'd given up.

FBI headquarters went along with this. So did Jim Holt and Jim Milburn. Holt remembered the time. "Our approach," he said, "and when I say our approach, I'm talking about Milburn and me, was to make sure we'd covered all the bases and narrowed it down to the best possible list. Even with what we had in the fall of 1992, we could not say these compromises were exclusively because of Ames. We had come so far, we wanted to make sure we gave the investigators as complete a report as we could. . . .

"It's easy to say in hindsight that Ames was the guy and we were crazy. Why wasn't something done quicker? But if you stop and look, what we had were some meetings with a Soviet who, by the way, was not an intelligence officer. We did have a lot of inflow of cash and we had his broad access to all these compromised cases that was damning on the face of it. But who was to say that the money didn't come from gambling, or smuggling of some sort, or from drugs? And we still hadn't nailed down the alleged wealth of his in-laws. You couldn't ignore that on the record, the CIA record, he had passed two polygraphs which specifically addressed unauthorized contacts and disclosures to foreign nationals. Finally, there were others on the list who could not be eliminated."

Tim Caruso came into Bryant's office. "Listen," he said, "this has been going on for close to nine years. We can afford another couple of months or so to be sure we've got the right person."

By the end of 1992, the bigot list was down to ten names. Two more months went by. "You're always fine-tuning, and maybe that's a drawback," Holt recalled. "There may have been the feeling that if we hang on, if we look at one more thing, or if we go over these records again, we'll see the thing that would enable us to say definitely that it's Ames and nobody else. I must say that Jean Vertefeuille and Sandy Grimes were convinced it had to be Ames."

On March 15, 1993, Caruso received an eighty-page draft report written by Milburn.

Now there were five names.

Rick Ames topped the list, and now not just alphabetically. But the four other candidates remained in the running. They could not be positively discounted—and to this day, Holt can't say whether one or more of them has something to hide.

But then, as far as the Playactor probe into the compromised cases was concerned, the last piece in the puzzle fell into place that made it all but certain Ames was the wanted man.

In the shambles that the KGB found itself in after the collapse of Communist rule, someone had finally been found who had access to the files of Directorate K in the First Chief Directorate. He did not know Rick's identity, only his code name, "Kolokol." "Kolokol" was in CIA counterintelligence. He had begun providing information in 1985. He had met his controller in Bogotá and, in the latter 1980s, in Rome. The source that the FBI had developed was a closely held secret, even from the investigating agents. He was still actively providing information about others who had been in the pay of Russian intelligence and may yet be surfaced as a witness in future prosecutions.

In the hope that Rick might crack at once, Caruso recruited agent Rudy Guerin from CI-7, an overseas espionage squad. Guerin was the best man Caruso knew of for an assignment like this. Rudy Guerin always smiled when he thought of the lectures at the FBI Academy in Quantico, Virginia, which said that when you were trying to break somebody down, you should always use an agent similar to the target in age, physical appearance, and so on. Guerin's greatest triumph was getting a retired Chinese-born CIA translator to confess he'd been spying for Beijing for thirty-three years. Since the FBI didn't have enough to arrest the translator, his *Miranda* rights did not have to be read. Guerin was sent in to see what he could do. So there was this skinny little redheaded Irish kid from Chicago's South Side confronting this venerable Chinese, who denied everything. Guerin kept trying to find an opening. Their conversation turned to values. Nothing was more important, the Chinese observed, than one's relationship with one's sons, of which he had two. Guerin let it pass and then, just as he was leaving, he said that he was going to have to question the sons about any involvement in their father's illegal acts.

"You wouldn't do that?"

"I'm sorry. It's my job."

"Please. I will tell you everything."

With Rick Ames, however, it was decided on second thought not to use this strategy. Rick was too slick. He'd dig in his heels and get a lawyer. This had to be pursued the hard way, buttoned down. And it wasn't going to be an overnighter.

That was when Bear Bryant at last opened the case on May 12, 1993, and then, twelve days later, summoned Les Wiser Jr. to his office late in the afternoon and asked him if he would like to head up the crucial last stage of the investigation. There'd be a new code name for it.

Nightmover.

8

All the CI squad agents at Buzzard Point had been cleared for the highest national security classification—sensitive compartmented information, which embraced specific code-worded top-secret projects and operations. Still, every agent associated with Nightmover had to undergo a new polygraph, even Les Wiser.

When Rudy Guerin was detached from his regular squad, his supervisor asked, "What's going on in there?"

"I can't tell you."

"What do you mean, you can't tell me?"

"Listen, I've got to take a poly. And that's the first question they'll ask me. Have I talked to anyone about this?"

After Bear Bryant opened the case on May 12, there was an overlap of about a month between Wiser and Tim Caruso in room 11610—between Playactor and Nightmover. Wiser needed time to wrap up some operations in the CI squad he was then heading. And

137

plans were already in motion that Tim Caruso had started.

Besides recruiting Guerin (as well as another debriefer, a burly agent named Mike Donner, the exact physical opposite of Guerin) in the hope of immediately cracking Ames, Caruso had drawn up a massive twenty-four-hour-a-day surveillance not only of Rick, but of some thirty intelligence officers known to be stationed in what was now the Russian embassy, any one or more of whom might be his local contact. All seventy of the so-called G's, officially the Special Support Group of the CI squads, experts highly trained in tailing suspects, would be mobilized. From all over the country, reconnaissance aircraft—the FBI had over a hundred of them—were being flown in. A special exemption had been granted by the Federal Aviation Administration so that these planes and helicopters could fly at night over urban areas without lights if need be.

At the last minute, however, after the initial rush of excitement had subsided, Caruso had big second thoughts. "Bear," he told Bryant, "I'm feeling more and more uncomfortable about this. We just don't have enough basic intelligence on Ames and how he operates. Surveillance should be like a surgeon's scalpel. This way, it's going to be a blunt instrument and we can blow everything. Let's call it off, at least until we get a better idea of where we are." Many of the pilots were already en route. "I don't think my name ranked very high with them," Caruso recalled. "I'm glad I didn't meet any of them personally."

But Bryant readily agreed. He'd had misgivings about the idea himself. He instructed Wiser about future surveillance. "Be judicious," he said. "If there's a choice, the choice is don't get burned. This is too important."

And later on, whenever J. R. Heard, the lead team

coordinator of the G's who worked on the Ames case, happened to bump into Bryant in an elevator at the Washington Field Office, the Bear wouldn't give him a jolly "Hi" or "How's it going?" He'd just growl, Heard remembered, "Don't get burned."

Bryant told Wiser that while Caruso would be returning to headquarters, he had persuaded Mike Anderson to stay on despite the career sacrifice he was making. Besides his intimate knowledge of how the old Directorate K operated out of the embassy, Anderson would be an invaluable bridge to what had gone on before in Playactor. "You're the lead agent on this, you're responsible," Bryant said, "but I want you to work with Mike as a partner."

Anderson and Caruso gave Wiser his initial rundown on what was known about Rick, including the fact that he had now been transferred to the CIA's Counternarcotics Center to get him into a less sensitive position. Then the CIA auditor Dan Payne was brought in. On an overhead projector, Rick's (and Rosario's) cash deposits that Payne had discovered flashed on the wall—ninety-two of them in all, totaling one million five hundred thirty-eight thousand six hundred and eighty-five dollars.

It was pointed out that right after Rick's unauthorized stopover in Caracas in October 1992, he had made "structured" cash deposits under ten thousand dollars that amounted to eighty-seven thousand dollars.

What about a narcotics tie-in? Wiser asked. Was it possible that Ames could have been selling information to the Colombian cocaine cartels? Had he been hired to launder money, washing it here in the States for drug dealers? Maybe there were other bank accounts.

It had all been considered, he was told. Jean Vertefeuille at the CIA had even raised the possibility of emerald smuggling. The world's finest emeralds came from Colombia. That, Wiser had to admit, was something he hadn't thought of. Besides, there were all those cash deposits Rick made right after his meetings, reported and unreported, with the Soviet diplomat Sergei Chuvakhin. For sure, Chuvakhin wasn't into dope.

You had to touch all the bases, though, Wiser believed. This was going to be his baby now. You had to think like an investigator. If you had to bet the farm, it undoubtedly was espionage, but it was important not to make a mistake and close off other avenues. "It was always important to me to keep an open mind," Wiser recalled. "I had to be convinced that this was what it seemed to be. You set that standard and then you can make the case."

And it was one thing to identify a suspect and quite another to prove it. Perhaps out at Langley, the feeling was we helped you get your man, next case, this one was over. But it wasn't, not by a long shot. As Mike Anderson put it to Wiser, "This guy looks pretty good. We think he's the guy. Now comes the hard part."

Wiser came away from these briefings thinking, Well, bottom line, this guy's good for something. He had an appreciation, moreover, that this Ames was pretty shrewd. Take the house cash purchase. Wiser put himself in Rick's shoes. If he went to get a mortgage loan on a house that cost that much, the bank would want a full review to make sure that there weren't any liens on the property. It would look at his salary and income tax returns. He'd have to fill out all sorts of forms explaining where the money was coming from, complete with detailed records that could be traced. In all probability, Rick hadn't wanted to do this, especially if it was dirty money.

Wiser decided that one of the first things he had to

do was bring in a bureau financial expert named Mike Mitchell. Before joining the FBI, the thirty-three-year-old Mitchell had been with the accounting firm Price Waterhouse.

Wiser showed him the deposit data that the CIA's Payne had provided. "You think there's money laundering here?"

"You've got to be kidding," Mitchell replied.

Mitchell was working at an FBI facility in Tysons Corner, Virginia, right by Langley, winding up a phase of the famous worldwide BCCI—the Bank of Credit and Commerce International—fraud scandal.

"Les called," Mitchell remembered, "and asked me to come in. First thing, I had to sign a little form saying that I had to give away my firstborn if I talked about the case I'm about to hear. In the beginning, I was not given the counterintelligence side of what was happening."

After receiving confirmation that structured criminal money laundering was obviously involved, Wiser told Mitchell, "Okay, let's go to talk to the Bear." It was Mitchell's first real experience with Bryant. "Bear said to tell him about myself and then he said, 'I only want people who are committed to this case. And we can't have any screw-ups.' 'Yes, sir,' is what I said."

Like the G's J. R. Heard, Mike Mitchell feared bumping into Bryant in an elevator at Buzzard Point. "Remember, Mitchell," he'd always say. "No screw-ups."

Mitchell started repeating everything Payne had done and far more. He wanted to go beyond the statements. And now he learned that besides the two accounts Rick maintained at the Dominion Bank of Virginia, he had still a third in the Washington area, at Riggs National. Mitchell paid special heed to the collection of credit cards Rick had. "Credit card information," he said, "is very valuable to us in counterintelligence because it allows us to place the target—in this instance, Ames—in a particular city or country based on the charge. I issued national security letters all over again. I skipped department stores because we didn't—maybe 'trust' is too harsh a word—but we didn't trust the security of a local store versus a big bank or national credit card company. I set a five-hundred-dollar minimum for checks and deposits. I wanted to see the actual deposit slips, whose handwriting they were in, and I wanted the teller's cash-in ticket to get the exact time and date to match them up with the meetings he had that Jim Milburn told me about. That was crucial if you ever have to go into court. I wanted to see the checks, too, for lead information. Who or what were they made out to? Any assets he may have purchased? Did he have a secret P.O. box? What other banks overseas was he using? I wanted the same thing for the wife—Rosario—to show that she was in this with him. I figured—worst-case scenario, if all else failed, if there wasn't supporting evidence that he was involved in espionage—we'd have him dead to rights on major income tax evasion and money laundering. We had structuring, we had mail fraud, and we had wire fraud from the Swiss accounts he had."

Tim Caruso and Mike Anderson also advised Wiser that FISA applications had been made for wiretaps and bugs. Established by law in 1978, FISA stood for the Foreign Intelligence Surveillance Act. Staffed by a single clerk, a FISA court met every two weeks at the Department of Justice. Rotating judges from federal district courts presided. At that time, applications were presented to the court by the Justice Department's counsel for intelligence policy and review, Mary C. Lawton. While Lawton herself had turned down requests, the court had never been known to refuse any of her recommendations. And she was recommending this one.

Taps were placed on Rick's home phone on June 11. They would be monitored at a command post at the Washington Field Office.

Wiser, meanwhile, assembled the G's for hands-on surveillance. The seventy G's who supported the field office's counterintelligence efforts ranged in age from twenty-four to sixty. They encompassed a variety of races and both sexes. Three teams, each working an eight-hour shift and consisting of eight men and women, would be regularly assigned to the Ames investigation. Among the team coordinators were John Powers, AKA "Hooker," a husky, onetime emergency medical services driver whose father had been a cop in Connecticut; Sherry "Pepper" Greene, a sexy African American who'd been a dancer; and "Preacher," softspoken Charles Payton, also African American, who had abandoned an early religious calling for a secular life that still enabled him to do what he considered God's work.

J. R. Heard, the lead G's coordinator for Nightmover, had the look of an aging hippie left over from Woodstock. Like all the G's, Heard had been trained at the FBI Academy at Quantico. Initially, they were given historical background about the threat from the Soviet Union, Soviet-bloc nations, and China. They got intensive training in communications and photography. Then there was foot surveillance. "You'd go off base. You'd have a target," he said. "You'd come back and explain what you saw. You saw someone put down a dead drop, or someone did a brush pass, or someone read a signal or put up a signal. And then you'd be debriefed by instructors playing the parts of hostile intelligence officers who would critique the training sessions, who'd say, 'I picked you out as surveillance because you were coming at me and suddenly you turned around,' or, 'I saw you twice in a ten-minute period.' "

And there was vehicular surveillance. How to run pursuits. To skid pan. What the enemy would do to shake off—or spot—a tail, making a right-hand turn from a center lane, signaling a right turn and immediately turning left, flipping into a U-turn, darting into a parking lot and driving right through it, shooting a traffic light just as it was turning red.

In surveillance, Heard said, "it's not so much what you look like, but what you *don't* look like. You can't always anticipate what the right clothes will be. The key is your demeanor. You can be in a suit and tie, jeans, a turban, and it's not going to matter. What counts is how well you're selling yourself, that you're not the FBI, the police, whatever. Like if I'm in a store ahead of you—most people think surveillance is *behind* them—it doesn't matter how I'm dressed. I got there before you. And if I can sell you that I'm shopping, having an argument with my girlfriend, you're not going to think I'm a problem even if you happen to see me again in the neighborhood a little later."

Les Wiser reiterated Bear Bryant's injunction: Be judicious. At first, there would only be spot surveillance to establish the nature of the beast. If the choice was between losing Rick and even the remotest chance of being spotted, let him go.

The first thing was to scout the neighborhood where Rick lived at 2512 North Randolph Street, North Arlington—white, upper middle class, what the G's called the country club set, the residents mostly professional people, doctors and lawyers, high-level government bureaucrats, senior corporate types, many retirees. Did residents walk around much? What time did they go to bed? Were there many dogs in the area? Were there neighborhood watch patrols?

.

While the immediate area was entirely residential, it was surrounded by major traffic corridors with a dozen ways Rick could get to them. So choke points were identified and numbered for quick radio communication, locations that he would have to pass no matter what route he took—a scenic overlook, a key intersection, a shopping mall, a church parking lot that would be a good observation post except on Sunday.

Patterns also had to be established for Rick. When did he leave for work? Did he always go the same way? Note was made that Rick could take two parallel main thoroughfares toward CIA headquarters, Glebe Road and Military Road. Whenever he rather than Rosario drove his son, Paul, to the Marymount University day care center, he elected Glebe. Otherwise he always took Military. Why? How did he normally depart Langley? What were his usual weekend driving habits? Rosario had a Honda. What time did she leave for her studies at Georgetown University? What routes did she take? What time did they turn in for the night?

Bear Bryant himself provided crucial assistance. He knew of a retired FBI agent who resided a few blocks away from Rick. As a matter of fact, he had been head of the neighborhood association. Rick and Rosario weren't notable one way or the other, he said. Not especially social, but by no means reclusive. They regularly attended association meetings. Rick said he was with the State Department. What everyone knew was how much Rick had paid for the house, the retired agent especially. It turned out that the same builder had put up his home and they were identical. Of course, he was quick to say, he had bought his home many years ago. It was nice to know what the going price was now. This gave the G's a chance to see what the layout was in Rick's house. What lights in what windows meant what.

What's more, the ex-agent said that there was a house practically around the corner from Rick that was for rent. Even better, neighbors were used to it being a transient, nonfamily rental. For the past six months, it had been taken by four corporate executives on temporary assignment in Washington. They had just moved out. It would be perfect as a collection place for a videocamera installed by FBI technicians on a telephone pole opposite Rick's house. To transmit pictures, a line could be run directly to the rental, monitoring Rick's movements in and out of the house when he wasn't under personal observation. And while it was the longest of long shots that a Russian intelligence officer would ever show up on the premises, there was always that chance.

The next problem was to find a tenant for the rental. Then Les Wiser heard of an agent in the field office who was getting divorced and had nowhere to live. It wasn't a tough sell. The agent, otherwise ignorant of what was happening, couldn't believe his luck. He was told that there would be a room in the house that he was not to enter and that he'd be having visitors. "Hey," he said, "the more the merrier." The lease was for a year.

By now, under national security provisions, Attorney General Janet Reno had signed a warrantless search-and-seizure authorization. In the back of everyone's mind was that sooner or later—if Rick Ames wasn't caught in the act of passing classified CIA documents to the Russians—a secret entry somehow was going to have to be made into his North Randolph residence, to see what might be squirreled away there and to place electronic microphones.

More technical surveillance was installed. On June 25, Rick's phone at Langley was tapped. His workspace in counternarcotics, room GVO 6, was in the basement of the same building, four elevator stops down from his old counterintelligence haunts. It was a commodious area, filled with divided cubicles, with two enclosed offices at one end. He had been relegated to one of the cubicles, where FBI technicians, from some distance away, also affixed a tiny videocamera aimed at his desk and computer. His current counternarcotics boss had been advised that Rick was an investigative target. Only he and Paul Redmond, the deputy chief of the Counterintelligence Center and Rick's agency nemesis, knew about the camera.

Nightmover's liaison with the G's was agent Dell Spry, who during the Playactor phase of the investigation had tenaciously reviewed unresolved compromises and later confirmed Rick's unreported trip to Caracas. Spry was asked to stay on. "They would have had to blast me out with dynamite," he said. "I was there for the duration." He was on hand when the camera went in, and it would be his thankless chore, along with his day duties, to retrieve the videotapes at Langley every night, hanging around until room GVO 6 was deserted, and then return home to fast forward them on his VCR to see what, if anything, had occurred that indicated espionage activity.

Two other Nightmover agents, Julie Johnson and Mike Degnan, had equally thankless tasks, monitoring the taps, "working the wires." Both had been agents less than two years. From the time they were kids, they'd wanted to get into law enforcement. Julie had devoured Nancy Drew mysteries as an eight-year-old and used Jell-O as fingerprint powder to solve imaginary crimes. Mike had gotten a degree in accounting to help him get into the FBI. Julie was a mother with a thirteen-month-old son when she left for Quantico and the FBI Academy. Her husband, a furniture maker, told her he'd care for the baby for the four months of training. "Do it," he said. "It's what you've always wanted."

Degnan hoped to get on a white-collar crime squad. Johnson wanted to work street crime. Instead, they ended up in counterintelligence, on Les Wiser's overseas espionage squad. The one thing Wiser knew about them was their dedication to the job. As newcomers, they'd been working wires anyway. "Hey," Julie said to Mike, "what's a few more shifts on the wire?" Besides, Wiser had said the case was major, one they would be proud to have been part of.

On the morning of July 1, when Julie Johnson checked the reels for the night before, she listened to a call being dialed at eleven P.M. from Rick's home. She heard breathing, which she recognized as Rosario's. The rings continued without an answer. Then a robotic voice announced that the Cellular One customer being called was unavailable or out of range. That surprised her. The G's hadn't reported seeing an antenna for a car phone on the Jaguar, so it meant Rick must have a cell phone. Then later that afternoon, a Thursday, Mike Degnan listened to a call from Rick to Rosario. "I'm on Massachusetts Avenue. All's well. I'll be home shortly."

At Langley, employees "badged" in and out on a computerized system. As often as not, the system malfunctioned. This time it didn't. Rick, as would be discovered to everyone's chagrin, had badged out early that same afternoon.

It was the downside of spot surveillance.

The great goal was to have the G's trail Rick to a dead drop, witness him load it, replace what he had left with a dummy package after photographing the contents or leave the original material there—depending on what Les Wiser wanted—and have FBI counterintelligence agents pounce on the Russian who came to collect it.

What Rick had done the night before was to mark

a new signal site he'd been given in Caracas—signal
site "Rose," the mailbox on the corner of Garfield
Road and Garfield Terrace, near Massachusetts Avenue—to alert his handlers that he was about to load its
companion dead drop, "Ground," a crevice under a
walkway bridge in Rock Creek Park bordering the
District of Columbia and Montgomery County in
Maryland. His "All's well" call to Rosario was to let
her know that he had revisited "Rose" and seen that
his chalk mark was erased. That meant his package of
documents had been retrieved.

The first rehabilitative step was to put a tap on
Rick's cellular phone. The second was a bit more
complicated. At Langley, once again only Paul Redmond and the chief of the Counternarcotics Center,
Dave Edgers, were in on it. As instructed, Edgers told
Rick that the FBI wanted to hear about the agency's
Black Sea Initiative, an agency-sponsored cooperative
effort aimed at interdicting heroin that was being
smuggled westward out of Afghanistan and Pakistan
across the southern Russian republics. Edgers said
that since this was Rick's specialized area, he couldn't
think of anyone better qualified to speak for the CIA.
Delighted to have been chosen, Rick got right to work
preparing his briefing. The morning it was scheduled,
Edgers lamented that his car was out of commission.
"No problem," said Rick. "We'll go in my Jag."

At FBI headquarters, Rick and Edgers were waved
through security and directed to park on a driveway in
the inner courtyard. As soon as they were inside the
building, the Jaguar was moved to a basement garage,
where FBI technicians went to work putting in a
beacon underneath the chassis. They had been practicing for a week, trying to find the right spot to avoid
detection, using similar models that had been seized
from a regional foreign-car dealer involved in a money-
laundering scheme. The concern was that Jaguars

were known to have circuitry breakdowns that often had them back in the shop. For that reason, the idea of also inserting a bug in the Jaguar's interior was dropped. All Wiser needed was to have some mechanic say, "Gee, Mr. Ames, look what I found."

Meanwhile, on the fourth floor at headquarters, other problems were occurring that no one had anticipated. Since the briefing had been set up through Division 5, then called the intelligence division, one of its conference rooms was pressed into service. And after Division 6 narcotics agents gathered there, unaware of what was afoot, agent Dell Spry posted himself outside the door.

Suddenly a Division 5 section chief came by and poked his head inside. "What are those Division Six guys doing here?" he demanded of Spry. "This is my conference room. I need it and I need it now. Who are you, anyway?"

He was CI, Spry blurted. From the field office.

"The field office? What the hell's going on?"

"Sir," Spry said. "Sir, I can't tell you. But believe me it's important, really important. I'll get my supervisor to get in touch with you. I just can't tell you myself."

At that, the section chief stalked off and Spry heaved a sigh of relief. When Les Wiser was filled in, he started to laugh. Then he stopped. A dreadful thought had come to him. Suppose the briefing had been called off? He could see Ames unexpectedly down in the courtyard yelling, "What happened to my car?"

At first, the beacon performed as advertised. It didn't pinpoint the precise whereabouts of Rick's Jaguar, but it did signal the general area he was in and the direction he was going. All at once, however, it stopped beeping. It took the G's several days of observation to figure out what was wrong. It was the circuitry. Whenever Rick turned on his lights or his windshield wipers, the beacon cut out. It wasn't the end of the world. The G's had a remote-control activator to get the beacon back on. To do this, though, you had to have direct line of sight and be close up.

And if you believed in omens, this one didn't augur well.

9

Rick would be the one who most often drove his son, Paul, to a school at Marymount University, where he had previously been in day care. Rosario had moved heaven and earth to enter the boy in an elite, expensive school in Alexandria, Virginia, called Burgundy Farms. It was the first step on the road to Harvard for him, she thought. But to her dismay and irritation, Paul had not done well there.

The first call to Rick would come in the morning around ten A.M.

"Was everything all right when you dropped my baby off?" Rosario would say day after day.

"Yes, honey."

"How was he?"

"He was fine."

"But how was he, really? Did he cry?"

"No, he was really fine. Quite happy."

"You're sure?"

"Yes, honey, don't worry."

She'd phone her mother in Bogotá, usually every other day.

"Mama, it's me. Just calling to see how you are."

"Oh, my Rosa, I don't know what to do. These bills I have, the electricity alone! You won't believe them. I want to go to Cartagena. It's been so long. But I don't see how I can afford it. And I must give something to the peasants on the farm." Cecilia was recovering from a broken hip. "It's a miracle that I can walk again," she told her daughter. "Can you speak to Rick about more money? It's so difficult to make ends meet."

"All right, I'll talk to him and see what I can do."

Her brother, Pablo, would call, collect.

It was impossible living at home with Mother, he said. He had a new girlfriend. They were looking for a place of their own.

To make this feasible, what he required more than anything right then was money for a new car.

Could Rick loan him eight hundred dollars?

Well, this certainly iced one item, Les Wiser thought as he learned of these conversations.

All Rick's money, Rosario's fabled inheritance, wasn't northward bound. Whatever cash flow there was, it was going south.

Rosario rarely spoke to her sister, Claudia, a doctor in Colombia with three children.

"You can't imagine the suffering I'm going through," she'd tell her. "How my head aches constantly. It's my sinuses. They're infected. And you can't believe my back spasms. Most mornings I can barely get out of bed. These doctors I have here simply don't know what they're doing. I need Colombian doctors."

Claudia was not all that sympathetic. She said that she didn't consider Rosario's medical ailments to be grave. She was sure that doctors in the States were professionally competent.

Cecilia was more consoling. "Oh, you poor thing. You're studying too hard and having to take care of the baby at the same time, it's too much. . . . Rosa, have you spoken to Rick about the money? We must have it just for the management and telephones of your properties in Cartagena, Bogotá, and that *guajira* [the farm]."

Rosario regularly called her best woman friend, a Colombian living in Germany. "My mother is driving me crazy. If it isn't one thing, it's another. And always it's money, money, money. You can't believe how overworked I am. I just don't know what to do. I'm so sick all the time, and you won't believe how Paul misbehaves. He's such a little brat. He won't listen to me. He won't eat his dinner. I'm at my wits' end."

Rosario's studies at Georgetown University, where she was pursuing a doctorate in philosophy, were in the afternoon. Around lunchtime, she'd phone Rick again. "I'm leaving now," she'd say. "Can you remember to bring home milk and bread? And let me see, there are some other things we need."

"Sure, honey. Listen, right now I'm a little busy."

"Well, fine! If you can't spare the time to talk to me, just fine!" And then she slammed down the receiver.

Later, she'd call back. "Are you ready to talk to me now? What have you going on in your life that you can't get things from the grocery store?"

Wine was acceptable at home for dinner. Rick was also permitted beer. He did most of his heavy drinking alone at lunch in CIA hangouts around Tysons Corner, minutes from Langley. Rosario called his cellular phone religiously in the evening, usually at five-fifteen, to make certain he wouldn't be stopping off at a bar for a few pops of vodka or Scotch.

"Where are you?"

"In the parking lot. I'm just leaving. I'll stop at Giant [a supermarket chain] and get the things you wanted."

"Do you remember everything? Did you write it down?"

"Yes, dear. Don't worry."

"I need some cash. Where is it?"

"On the second shelf in my closet study."

"By the way, I spoke to Mother today. You know her maid, Elsa. She fell down the stairs or something and Mother feels obligated to pay her medical bill. I told her you would help out."

She was forever on the phone to department stores like Bloomingdale's, I. Magnin, and Nordstrom. She knew sales personnel at each of them. They had all her measurements.

"This is Mrs. Ames. I just got your new catalog. I love those beige cashmere sweaters. I'll take three of them."

"How are you? This is Rosario Ames. Send me two pairs of those Chanel shoes. Yes, the ones with the cross straps. In brown, of course."

"Is the new Calvin Klein line in? I loved that ensemble you showed me. The slacks and that sweater and the belt and shoes. Just charge them to my account."

"You remember that tan leather coat? The one for a thousand dollars. I wasn't sure about it, but now I am."

Her inner tension would explode at the slightest provocation.

For a coloring book, Paul had wanted to use only an orange crayon.

"No," she said. "Do this picture properly. You have to use different colors."

Then she saw that he had colored outside the lines. "No, no!" she screamed. "You're so stupid. You're just a stupid little child."

They were having dinner. Paul wanted to go to the bathroom. "Mommy, please turn on the light for me," he said. "I have to go to the potty."

"You can do it yourself."

"I don't want to. It's dark in there."

"You're such a 'fraidy cat. A little sissy. There's nothing to be scared of."

"Daddy, *please!*"

Finally, Rick got up and switched on the light.

Paul was to go to a birthday party for one of his school friends.

Rosario gave him paper and a pencil. "Here," she said, "make your own card. Copy what Mommy printed for you. Happy Birthday from Paul."

Paul reversed the "r" in birthday.

"Rick," Rosario shouted. "Come in here and look at this. In Bogotá, every child knows how to read and write at Paul's age. I can't believe this. We're spending all this money sending him to this school and he doesn't even know his letters yet."

She turned her wrath on the boy. "You're so stupid!" And she stormed out of the room. "It's so embarrassing. We'll stop on the way and buy a card."

"Let's try again, son," Rick said quietly to the sobbing Paul. "You can do it. But Mommy's right. You have to pay attention to your letters."

Sometimes a completely different Rosario would materialize.

On Sunday mornings, Rick would make breakfast for her and bring it up to the bedroom on a tray.

Paul would come in to have breakfast with them and to watch cartoons while they read the papers.

"Oh, how's Mommy's darling little boy?" she'd coo. "Come up here on the bed next to her and give her a big kiss. Tell Mommy how much you love her. You look so handsome. Did you have sweet dreams?"

"Hi, honey, how'd it go today?" Rick said.

"I'm exhausted, absolutely exhausted. I'm simply stressed out. You know how hard I'm working on my thesis. The professors are never available when you want to see them. It's really disgraceful."

Rick's favorite television program was *N.Y.P.D. Blue*.

"How can you watch such a dumb show?" she asked.

"I like it. It's really well done."

Only once did Rick talk back to her. He was attending a narcotics conference in Turkey.

He was clearly drunk when she called.

"Have you been drinking?"

"No, I haven't. You're always so rude to me. Why do you just call me to yell at me all the time? You really enjoy it, don't you?"

She hung up on him.

When he phoned her the next day to apologize, she hung up on him again.

Nelson, an Ecuadoran gardener and handyman Rosario employed, along with two Latin American maids, gave her a chance to vent her anti-American spleen.

She normally paid them in cash, but once she

wrote a check to reimburse Nelson for some out-of-pocket expenses.

Since he didn't have any identification when he went to cash the check, the bank called her to verify that it was all right.

She took it out on Rick. "How dare they do that? It's my check. I pay the people I want to pay. If he was American, they never would have questioned him."

"Honey," Rick said, "they were only practicing good bank security."

"No! It was because he was a Latin American person. Americans think they can treat us like dirt. They are the rudest, crudest people on earth. That's why I think I'm having such trouble with Paul. He saw that *Dennis the Menace* video. It's things like that, *your* culture, that have corrupted him. I can't wait until I get him back to Colombia."

Never once did she express a word of concern that Rick was betraying his country—and hers as well, since she had become a U.S. citizen.

At the Washington Field Office, Les Wiser had requested Rick's last CIA polygraph, not only the chart but the audiotape that went with it. While no one was claiming that polygraphs were a hundred percent accurate, the FBI believed in their efficacy. A study of twenty thousand bureau polygraphs showed a failure rate of less than one percent. It depended on how a polygraph was administered and how good the examiner was in interpreting the results.

Wiser had the field office's top polygrapher, a laconic southerner named Barry Colvert, review Rick's test, the one that had been marked "incomplete" prior to the second, and ultimately successful, try.

"What do you think?" Wiser asked.

"Oh, my, you've got a problem here," Colvert said. "This fellow flunked it cold. Look at this."

> Question: "Have you had contact with a foreign national that you want to hide from the CIA?"
> Answer: "No."

"Talk about deception," Colvert said. "He's having just about everything 'cept a heart attack!"

For Wiser, Colvert's reaction made it even more frustrating that the FBI had missed the drop Rick had made on the first Thursday in July. According to Jim Milburn, who was a consultant on Nightmover, if the Russians were adhering to their normal cycle, it would be another two or three months before the next drop took place.

It was going to be a long, hot—and dry—summer.

Wiser and the Nightmover agents tried to look at the bright side. Any lingering doubts that Rick Ames was the man they were after had vanished.

First, there'd been the call itself that Rick made on his cellular phone on Massachusetts Avenue following the July drop.

Second, there was the analysis of Rick's deceptive polygraph.

Third, the idea of Rick's money coming from a family inheritance in Colombia was demonstrably a myth.

Fourth, at Langley, Rick had been promoted from the bullpen in the Counternarcotics Center to an office of his own. Actually he'd been doing a quite creditable job. The hidden videocamera went with him, and in the nightly runthrough of the tapes collected by agent Spry, Rick was seen working at his computer, inserting and extracting floppy disks and putting them in his briefcase.

But there was no smoking gun.

They just couldn't sit there and wait, Wiser thought. How were they ever going to nail down this case? He yearned to do a trash cover. Go through Rick's garbage. Wiser himself had made his first arrest doing just that. He always remembered spreading newspaper on his desk and dumping out the refuse and trying not to breathe too much—going through chicken bones and rotting vegetables—while another agent stood by with a spray can as maggots wriggled away.

Now it was a lot more sophisticated. Special Response Teams, volunteers from the G's, routinely handled trash covers, equipped with safety coveralls, surgical gloves, tongs, breathing masks. They were trained as well in proper evidence collection—not to put a wet piece of paper in a sealed plastic container, for instance, which could cause it to mildew.

But a trash cover where Rick lived would be as difficult as it could get, a well-to-do neighborhood, homes close together, generally older residents, watchful, who could be expected to be on the alert for any unusual activity. What's more, refuse collection was highly organized. The county did it. Pickups were once a week. And the garbage cans weren't just any cans. You had to use large, specially designed containers with wheels that the county supplied. Each home got only one container, which had to be ready at the curb on a regularly scheduled collection day. The rest of the week, it was kept on your property. Rick's container was on the garage side of his house behind a wood fence with a locked gate at least forty feet from the street. Even worse, his trash could not be simply hauled away. Like everyone else on Randolph Street, he trundled out his container in the evening, but the garbage trucks didn't get around to his block before ten A.M., giving him ample time in the morning to decide to toss in something else and discover that the container was empty.

The biggest hurdle of all, however, was Bear Bryant. It was too risky. "I'm an insomniac," he said. "I'd hear something like that in a minute during the night. Suppose someone like me lives across the street from Ames?"

Then Mike Mitchell, on his own still pursuing Rick's financial assets and dealings, said, "I'd really like a trash cover. He could be throwing away paper we could use, a mutual fund receipt, a stock buy confirmation, an envelope from some bank we don't know about. Names."

Wiser told J. R. Heard, the lead coordinator with the G's, to check out the neighborhood at night. "Find out exactly when Ames goes to bed. Where his bedroom is. What neighbors stay up late. How well lighted is the street? If you don't think there's close to a hundred percent chance to pull it off, we'll forget about it."

Garbage collection for North Randolph Street was Wednesday morning. So at eleven o'clock on a sultry Tuesday night in August, in the company of his Siberian husky to see if any dogs roaming loose could be a problem, and with Dell Spry, the liaison agent for the G's, Heard started strolling around the area. It looked good. Sidewalks were deserted. Only an occasional car. The biggest sound was the hum of air conditioners. Most of the homes were dark. There was a dim light shining through one of Rick's upstairs windows. His container was in place at the curb, its handles neatly turned out. An hour later, when Heard and Spry did a second tour, the upstairs light was still on. Heard guessed right. It must be for the kid in case he had to go to the bathroom. On one of the taps, he recalled, the wife was complaining about how the boy was afraid of the dark.

"Hey, Les," Heard said. "It's real doable."

There remained Bear Bryant, though.

One of the Nightmover agents said, "Why don't we do a trash cover on Bear? Bag his stuff and be dramatic. Show it to him the next day and say, 'You mean you didn't hear anything?' That should convince him."

Everybody laughed. Nervously.

"Ah, you know, guys," said Wiser with a straight face, "I don't think going through the boss's garbage is such a great idea. He might not find it so funny."

Finally, with Mike Anderson and Mitchell backing him, Wiser persuaded Bryant to let them try it.

"Just remember when you're all tripping around in the dark out there," the Bear said, "this is the most important U.S. espionage case the FBI has ever had."

The plan was to spirit off Rick's container during the middle of the night as it sat on the curb, rush it to the secret site that the G's worked out of in northern Virginia—the code name for it was "Hill Street," after the television show—sift through the contents, and return the container before daybreak. The time frame for the operation would be an hour and a half, the pickup at two A.M., the return no later than three-thirty. The problem was how to get a replacement container for the interim period. Enlisting the cooperation of the county carter was too dicey. Many of the workers on the trucks were Hispanic, a number of them Colombian. It was more than possible that Rosario had met and chatted with one of them. All Nightmover needed was for him to mention that the FBI had come by and requested a container. Whatever else she was, Rosario was no fool.

Then Les Wiser thought of the agent living in the house that had been rented around the corner to collect the video footage from the camera aimed at the front of Rick's home. He had the agent report that his container had been stolen. Another container was delivered to him the next day.

The G's began intensive practice with it. The substitute container was filled with newspapers to get everyone used to the weight. A container belonging to a relative of one of the G's who lived in Arlington was used as a stand-in for Rick's container during the practice sessions. The van was black with sliding side doors. Four G's were in the rear of the van. The driver would say, "Door!" Two of the G's would leap out, toting the dummy container. The other two were right behind them, grabbing the container at the curb. As soon as it was lifted out of the way, the dummy container was put in its place.

During an actual trash cover, there was always a walk-by first. There was a separate receptacle that Rick brought out for items to be recycled. Where had he placed it? There might also be a potted plant he had thrown out that was leaning against the container or perhaps boxes that merchandise had come in. As the van glided up North Randolph Street, a chase car with Mike Mitchell and Dell Spry in it would trail behind. In case a neighbor became suspicious or called the cops, they would be on hand to identify themselves as FBI agents and explain that there was nothing to be alarmed about. As it happened, however, this never occurred.

Les Wiser came by the "Hill Street" site around midnight for the initial trash cover. "We were sitting around eating pizza and watching a movie," Heard recalled. "But we had our game faces on. Les was real calm. He just wished us luck. He said he knew we could do it."

The time for the initial exchange of containers was twelve seconds, the next one eleven.

Rick's container was rushed to "Hill Street," where other G's were waiting. There were two long

makeshift tables of plywood set up on wooden horses
with sides about six inches high. Wet trash went on
one, dry on the other. But before anything else was
done, Polaroids were taken of what was inside the
container, so when everything was put back, the top
part at least would look the same.

Aesthetically, Rick's garbage could have been
worse. Although Rosario had a full shelf of gourmet
cookbooks, meals were mostly pasta and broiled
meats. Paul's diet was largely "beanie weenies." Bags
of urine-stained pull-up disposable diapers indicated
that he remained a serious bedwetter. There was a
plethora of cigarette butts. Rosario, as well as Rick,
was a chain smoker. A lot of female toiletries and
medications. Empty bottles of wine, more of beer. An
occasional bottle of Scotch or vodka. Dozens of fashion magazines, shopping catalogs, and clothes sales
tags.

There were three trash covers in August. Mike
Mitchell got some financial tidbits, a Hilton Hotel bill
confirming he'd been in Caracas, but nothing earth-
shaking.

Sooner or later, something had to give, Les Wiser
kept telling himself. "Come on, God," he'd whisper,
drifting off to sleep, "give us a break."

The last week in August, Rick was overheard announc-
ing to Rosario, "We're going to Miami." That instantly got everyone's attention. Rick never made
decisions like this. Rosario was the dominant voice in
the household.

What was up? Bogotá, Caracas, or Mexico City
were only a short flight from Miami. Was he going to
meet a handler in from Moscow? Deliver a major
package? Dutifully, Rosario was heard making reser-
vations at the Doral resort hotel. The first thing she

asked about was whether there were day care facilities for a child.

FBI technicians wired the room that Rick, Rosario, and Paul would be staying in. The Doral management agreed to cooperate. It involved the highest national security.

Eight agents, including the phone monitors, Mike Degnan and Julie Johnson, were booked into a nearby hotel. For Degnan and Johnson, it was particularly tough. Mike's favorite uncle had died the day before he was to leave, and his wife would have to attend the funeral without him. And the day they did leave, Julie's baby son came down with a high fever. Her husband, Nick, said he would watch over him. If his condition worsened, he'd just call her and she'd come back. A three-room suite was reserved for the agents, seven males in two of the rooms and the third for Julie. Julie was a handsome woman who looked as though she'd just come off a Colorado ski slope. "What's our cover story?" she joked. "A family reunion of seven guys and their slut maid?"

Rick and family arrived in Miami on August 30. They went to art galleries, visited the aquarium, strolled around Miami's South Beach, spent hours at poolside. Rosario was in the beauty salon every day to have her hair washed and waved. "Please stay away," she would warn Paul. "Don't mess up Mommy's hair."

It turned out that all Rick had in mind was a vacation. At night, he would read biblical passages to Paul to get him asleep. He had a sonorous, cadenced voice, and Degnan, listening to it, often found himself starting to doze off before Paul did. There was no Caracas or Bogotá—or Mexico City, for that matter.

Julie Johnson reflected what they all thought.

"What a bummer," she said.

Rick returned to Washington on Labor Day, September 6.

The next afternoon, Bear Bryant summoned Wiser. He told Wiser to call off the trash cover. The reason was a book titled *The FBI,* by Ron Kessler, which had just been published. Kessler, a onetime *Washington Post* investigative reporter, had previously written *Inside the CIA,* a well-received history of the agency. No one doubted that he had access within the bureau. And in the spring of 1993, as he was ready to sign off on his galleys, Kessler learned that the FBI was getting information from a former KGB "employee" about Americans who had been spying for the Soviet Union. "So specific was the information," he wrote, "that the FBI was quickly able to establish the source's credibility."

Although Kessler was not aware of the Nightmover investigation into Rick Ames, he was, as Bryant well knew, basically correct about a KGB source. The fact that a KGB defector had put the finishing touches on Rick—and was fingering others—was a closely held secret. Bryant said that Ames was sure to read or hear about Kessler's book and would go on full alert. In any event, they couldn't chance it. The trash cover had to be shut down. If anyone asked why, Bryant said, "just tell them it's because of the book and it doesn't matter whether what's in it is true or not."

Newspapers, newsmagazines, and television all carried reports about what Kessler wrote. Both the bureau and the agency made efforts, partially successful, to downplay its significance or pooh-pooh it outright.

But Bear Bryant was right. Rick did know about the book. An FBI agent was now on liaison duty at the CIA Counterintelligence Center and Rick was always dropping by. "What do you think about the

Kessler book?'' he asked. "Is the source you have really that good?"

The agent, forewarned, replied with a shrug, "I wish we had one. I don't know where reporters get this stuff. I guess they just make it up. And you can't do anything about it."

"Yeah, you're right," Rick said, apparently satisfied.

Earlier in the month, on September 1, forty-four-year-old Louis J. Freeh was sworn in as the new director of the FBI. Although it hadn't affected Nightmover, the bureau had been in disarray for months. Judge William Sessions, Freeh's predecessor, after months of fighting charges that he had misappropriated government funds for his private use, was dismissed at last by President Clinton.

Freeh's appointment was widely applauded, especially by FBI street agents, the heart and soul of the bureau. After getting his law degree, Freeh had been a street agent himself, the happiest years of his life, he was quoted as saying. Ever since he was a kid growing up in New Jersey, he had always wanted to be an FBI agent. He'd become disenchanted only after he was transferred to FBI headquarters and got caught up in bureaucratic red tape and what he considered to be senseless paperwork. He quit the bureau and joined the U.S. Attorney's Office for the Southern District of New York as a prosecutor. In 1991, he was named a federal judge.

It was as an assistant U.S. attorney that he became a legendary figure in law enforcement. He was dispatched by the Department of Justice from New York to Atlanta, Georgia, to take control of an investigation that was going nowhere—a federal judge and a prominent civil rights lawyer had been the victims of mailbomb murders. Other federal judges had received threats that they were in line for the same fate.

Eventually, a malcontent, Walter J. Moody Jr., was arrested for the murders and held in jail for trial. Still, the evidence against him was not airtight. One day Freeh ordered an application for a bug to be placed in Moody's cell.

"But Louie," he was told, "what good is that going to do? He's in there alone."

Freeh, however, in reading thousands of pages of investigative documents, had found a single, revelatory sentence that escaped everybody's notice. Moody had the habit of talking to himself. It would cap the case against him. Shortly thereafter, Moody was caught muttering in his cell, "Kill those damn judges . . . I shouldn't have done it. *Idiot!*"

Two weeks before he was officially sworn in, but after he was confirmed by the U.S. Senate, Freeh was taken aside by Floyd Clarke, then the FBI's acting director. Floyd said that the bureau had a big case going, a major espionage penetration of the CIA.

Freeh's oath of office was administered by his personal hero, the retired federal judge from Alabama, Frank Johnson Jr., who in one of his first judicial rulings—the historic Rosa Parks case—had declared his state's bus segregation laws unconstitutional. The day afterward, Clarke filled him in on all the details of the Ames investigation: Playactor, the last-minute sensitive corroboration that had come in, Nightmover. "We don't have a case yet," Clarke said. "But we're confident we're getting close."

Freeh wanted to know if Nightmover was getting everything it needed. Manpower? Money? The FBI didn't need another Edward Lee Howard.

No problem.

Was the CIA cooperating?

"Yes, *finally*," Clarke said.

As Freeh embarked on a sweeping reorganization of the bureau, the most drastic since its founding, shifting some six hundred desk-bound agents, half of them at headquarters, out to combat crime in the streets, he instituted an eight A.M. daily meeting with his top management. After each of them, he would receive a private update on Ames from Douglas Gow, previously head of Division 5 and now an associate deputy director.

On Wednesday afternoon, September 8, Gow came into Freeh's office, all aglow. "This could be it on Ames," Gow said. "We think it's coming down in the next twenty-four hours."

10

The initial tip-off was on Tuesday, September 7.

Rick started calling for weather forecasts on his phone at Langley.

Then, on Wednesday, in one of Rosario's endless daily calls to him, she reminded Rick that the next day Paul would be starting at the Burgundy Farms Country Day School in Alexandria.

"Can you drive Paul to where the school bus picks him up tomorrow?" she said. "I have so much work to prepare before I see my professor."

"Yes, but I have to go out really early first."

"What for? What do you have to do?"

"Have you forgotten? I told you, I have that errand I have to do."

"Oh, one of those?"

"Yes. Don't worry, though. I'll be back in plenty of time for Paul."

At the field office, in the Nightmover room, everyone agreed that this had to be it. Rick was either going to lay down a drop or set a signal for one. What's more, it was a Thursday. The drop that they had

missed on the first of July was also on a Thursday.
According to Jim Milburn, the Russians faithfully
hewed to a regular pattern.

Les Wiser told Bear Bryant. Doug Gow at headquarters was immediately informed. Gow had made it
abundantly clear that he wanted to keep the new FBI
director abreast of every development in the case.

Wiser told Dell Spry to have the G's ready at 6:00
A.M. This was to be a full-press surveillance. Every
choke point Ames might pass had to be covered. This
time, he couldn't be lost.

At home, Thursday morning, Wiser woke up with
a start. He looked at his bedside clock. It was 4:30
A.M. He began fretting. Should he have had the G's
out earlier, say, at 5:30? Yesterday, 6:00 A.M. had
seemed so reasonable. Well, it was too late to do
anything about it now.

And six o'clock would have been fine—except that
the G's worked on a different schedule from agents.
When an agent was ordered to be somewhere at a
given time, it meant being there, on the spot, working.
For the G teams, however, it just meant the time to
assemble at their "Hill Street" site preparatory to
going out on the road for an eight-hour shift. Spry
hadn't realized this. He'd never been in this sort of
situation before.

The first G to arrive at North Randolph Street
did a drive-by at 6:35 A.M. He immediately sensed
something was wrong. Instead of being garaged,
Rick's Jaguar was sitting in his driveway. The G went
straight to the house where the videotapes were collected. And saw the bad news. The tape showed
Rick backing out of his garage. The time on the tape
registered 6:03. The tape also showed Rick returning.
The time was 6:33. Whatever Rick had done was done.
And it had taken him exactly half an hour to do it.
Rick had in fact laid down a horizontal chalk line at

signal site "Rose," the mailbox on the corner of Garfield Road and Garfield Terrace, a quick trip across the Potomac River with no traffic at that hour.

When J. R. Heard called the Nightmover number to explain what happened, he got Rudy Guerin. "Hey, he's already been out," Heard said.

"Shit," Guerin said. He had told Spry to start the surveillance earlier.

It was only the beginning of a day of unrelieved horror. "Black Thursday," it would be called.

When Rick was observed leaving later with his son, the beacon wasn't working in the Jaguar. And the G's didn't have a remote-control activator. Both gadgets were on the fritz. The day before, they were supposed to have been fixed. But on that Thursday morning, when the G's on surveillance duty went to look for them, they weren't in their proper drawer. And because of the urgency of the day, nobody had time to look for them.

Les Wiser was furious. At what had occurred and at himself. For Wiser, the first thing was to find out what the problem had been. That was when he learned about the misunderstanding concerning the time start for the G's.

Wiser huddled with Mike Anderson and Jim Milburn. Both of them were experts on how the K directorate line officers operated in Washington. Even with the great shake-up in the KGB at Moscow Center, they weren't going to change their spots.

"What do you think Ames was doing?" Wiser asked.

Milburn said that he was pretty certain Rick had been laying down a signal for a drop, not making the drop itself. Ames had been gone for only thirty minutes. The Russians, from the heyday of the KGB till now, were creatures of habit. They had always favored dead drops in Maryland's Montgomery County, usually in wooded rural areas you had to get to by walking. It didn't seem likely that Rick would have had enough time to load one.

Mike Anderson made the point that a dead drop was usually loaded the same day a signal was set. That way, a Russian intelligence officer would see it driving to the embassy downtown. All was not lost, Anderson said. Ames would probably make his next move later that afternoon or early evening.

Rick had to be covered at Langley. That presented another problem. The agency had refused to let the G's inside its gates. The security office said that it simply couldn't let all kinds of people wander around. There were three ways in and out of the CIA. One was the main entrance on Route 123 toward McLean. There was a back egress leading to Turkey Run Road. A third curved steeply down to the George Washington Memorial Parkway, which ran parallel to the Potomac River. Rick always used the Route 123 gate.

Worse yet, the G's could not park outside any of the gates. Not six months before, a Pakistani had gunned down people at the main gate with automatic fire. Nor could the G's identify themselves to anyone outside the Washington Field Office. That was absolutely forbidden. They never even were seen at FBI headquarters.

They would have to keep moving back and forth past the gates. There was an Exxon station on Route 123 they could use and a scenic overlook on the parkway, but that was about it. Dell Spry was stationed at Langley. As soon as he saw Ames departing, he was to phone the command post at the field office.

Over a lunchtime sandwich, Wiser and Anderson decided more backup was required under the circumstances. An FBI reconnaissance plane would take to the air, circling over Langley, in communication with the G's. Just then, Wiser was ordered to appear on the double at FBI headquarters.

Douglas Gow, the associate deputy director, was steaming. He had gotten a call from the CIA's new director, James Woolsey. "Don't your people know how to make a surveillance?" Woolsey snapped.

Wiser attempted to explain the unfortunate circumstances of the morning and, echoing Mike Anderson, said that the day wasn't over. It still all might work out.

It better, said Gow.

Inside Langley, shortly after four P.M., Dell Spry saw Rick come out of his office, exit the building, and walk toward the parking lot. He rushed to a phone and called the Nightmover command post at the field office.

Mike Degnan, on duty there, notified J. R. Heard in his car. "He's leaving," Degnan said. But Degnan could not tell Heard which way out Rick would take. And at least five critical minutes had elapsed.

Suddenly more disaster struck.

The radio system that the G's used depended on a repeater dish on a tower in northern Virginia to enhance communications. A bird had chosen that hour to smash into the dish, knocking it out of commission. The cars with the G's patrolling the Langley perimeter could barely make out one another, much less Heard, who immediately sped toward Langley. But it was too late.

Rick had wheeled out of a CIA parking lot, using the parkway exit. Traffic on it was already heavy and moving fast. Unprepared for him, a G in a car parked on a grassy shoulder, a white Chevrolet Caprice similar to the unmarked cars that the police had, never saw him. And Rick turned off the parkway, crossing the Potomac over Chain Bridge, before reaching the scenic overlook.

There was a final, disheartening surveillance failure.

The backup FBI reconnaissance plane that Wiser had been counting on as a last resort was unable to get off the ground. That Thursday afternoon, commercial aircraft coming into Washington's National Airport were being routed directly over Langley. It was the busiest flight time of the day. A jet was landing every two or three minutes. There was no way that a light plane could maneuver around freely under those conditions.

At five o'clock, J. R. Heard parked near Rick's home. A couple of minutes or so later, one of the G's team leaders, John "Hooker" Powers, drove past Heard and stopped around the corner. For the first time all afternoon, they were close enough to communicate by radio. Ten minutes afterward, "Hooker" radioed, "Here he comes." And then Heard watched Rick Ames pull into his driveway and saunter into the house. He had been gone for an hour, but where, nobody knew. Heard noticed that Rick left the Jaguar outside instead of going into the garage. He isn't through for the day, Heard thought.

He called field headquarters to report the news. And was transferred to agent Mike Donner, who, along with Rudy Guerin, had been chosen early on to debrief Rick during those halcyon days when it was hoped that Rick Ames would quickly crack. Donner had stayed on with Nightmover and now Wiser decided to make him liaison with the G's.

"What's your situation?" Donner asked.

Heard told him about the trouble with the radios. "We need to get that repeater on the tower fixed right away."

Twenty minutes later, Donner called back. "It's done."

"I get the feeling," Heard said, "that he's not in for the night."

Donner replied that he was right. In a phone intercept earlier in the day, Rosario had told Rick not to forget the parent/teacher meeting that night at the Burgundy Farms school. It was scheduled for seven-thirty. "Les says to stay with him, all-out," Donner said. "Maybe this day isn't over yet."

By then, the missing remote-control devices to activate the beacon on the Jaguar had been located at the "Hill Street" site. "Get one over to me pronto," Heard said.

At seven P.M., when Rick and Rosario got in the car, the beacon was activated. Heard trailed leisurely behind. He knew where they were going. He saw them turn off Telegraph Road in Alexandria toward the school and enter the big circular driveway. He didn't follow them in. There was a guard, and alone, without wife or child, he might be stopped and questioned. So he turned back on Burgundy Road, parked, and waited.

About nine-thirty, the Jaguar went past him. Heard didn't have to reactivate the beacon. It was working perfectly. Ahead of him, and Rick, four other G cars were in position. Heard checked with them by radio. Their scanners were fine.

Rick headed back on the parkway. When he got to the Memorial Bridge interchange, instead of continuing on toward Arlington, he drove into Washington. Well, well, Heard thought, what do we have here? Then, again, maybe they were simply going into Georgetown for drinks and dinner. But Rick turned up 23rd Street past Georgetown, went left on Massachusetts Avenue, and drove north on it past the vice president's residence at the Naval Observatory.

Suddenly, he made a hairpin right on Garfield Road, heading south. Heard dropped back, letting a couple of cars go between him and Rick. There were several right-hand turns off Massachusetts that Rick could have made to get to Garfield. Maybe he was being careful, making sure he wasn't followed. Right where they were, Garfield inclined down for nearly a mile and Rick would have a clear view behind him in his rear vision mirror.

At the end of the incline, there was a rise and fall again. When Heard went over the rise, Rick was nowhere in sight. Now he understood why Rick had taken this route. On the other side of the rise, there was a confusing four-way intersection, a street to the left, two more angling off to the right, and straight ahead a continuation of Garfield Road, but with only two lanes instead of four. Still, the beacon showed that Rick was nearby.

Heard took the immediate left. He radioed the other G cars to divide up the remaining possibilities. The one that kept going straight on the two-lane part of Garfield spotted Rick stopped at the corner of a cul-de-sac called Garfield Terrace. Then Rick drove into the cul-de-sac. The G kept on for another block, turned around, and parked. He saw the Jaguar come out of the cul-de-sac and pause again at the corner before Rick gunned the car and returned directly to North Randolph Street.

J. R. Heard and "Hooker" drove into the Garfield Terrace cul-de-sac. The only possible place for a signal site was an unlikely big magnolia tree with drooping branches. There were too many houses around for a dead drop. They returned to the corner, where there was a telephone pole, a yellow "No Exit" sign, and a blue postal mailbox. They were searching for something, when in fact there was nothing. Rick had come by to make sure the chalk sign he had put down in the morning had been erased, showing that the dead drop he'd made in the afternoon had been cleared.

J.R. videotaped the scene. In the morning, when John Lewis, the assistant special agent in charge of the field office, saw it, he said, "It's got to be the mailbox. The Russians love mailboxes." So at least a signal site had been pinpointed.

That Thursday night, however, Wiser was crushed. He feared that he would be taken off Nightmover. In the end, no matter how you looked at it, he had to take the heat. He was the responsible agent. Word had already drifted down that Louis Freeh was an unhappy man. And it didn't take much of an imaginative leap to conclude what that might mean.

Freeh, in reality, was far less upset than his top management people. "These things happen. You win some and you lose some," he said. Then he started reminiscing about a big Mafia case he'd run in New York. An important Cosa Nostra meeting was going to take place at an unknown location. A certain mafioso was sure to attend. He was tailed. The leadership of a major organized crime family could be decimated as a result. But the mafioso had neglected to fill his gas tank and ended up being stuck on a country road in the middle of the night without ever making the meeting. Ergo, no bust.

Over the weekend, Wiser met with Anderson at the field office to pick up the pieces and to sum up what had been learned. Obviously, the technical snafus were unavoidable.

They noted that Rick had taken only seventy minutes to load his dead drop and that there was a lot of traffic. Assuming he'd gone into Montgomery County, that meant he wasn't engaging in any extraordinary, time-consuming maneuvers to throw off possible surveillance. So he wasn't worried about it.

The fact that Rosario had been with him in the car

indicated that she knew what he was doing. They'd have to keep closer tabs on her.

The time frame for the drop to have been unloaded was roughly between five and nine-thirty P.M. Videotapes of the Russian embassy and the Mt. Alto compound were reviewed. The movements of one KGB K line officer fit the bill. From then on, he would receive special attention.

They also now knew that there was a signal site at the corner of Garfield Road and Garfield Terrace, probably the mailbox. The resident of one of the homes across the street was approached and agreed to allow a camera to be installed to record the scene night and day.

Still, it was slim pickings compared with the might-have-been.

"We only have one way to go," Wiser said.

"Yeah," Anderson replied. "Up."

Wiser told Anderson that J. R. Heard had the best comment of all. Look, Heard had said, surveillance wasn't a science. It was an art form.

On Saturday, Bear Bryant found Wiser and Anderson huddled in the tiny command post where the phones were monitored.

"How's it over at headquarters?" Wiser asked.

"They want twenty-four-hour surveillance, starting now."

"That's not warranted. Why risk it? He isn't going to do anything more right away. The more we heat up any surveillance, the greater the chance that someone in the neighborhood will catch on. And if Ames doesn't pick up on it eventually, maybe the Russians will. How do we know they aren't keeping an eye on him?"

"I agree," Bryant said. "Don't worry. I'll get headquarters off your back." And as if he sensed that Wiser was apprehensive about being removed from the investigation, Bryant added that the new director of the FBI was being pretty cool about what had happened.

There would be, as a matter of fact, a polite, if icy, exchange between CIA director Woolsey and Freeh.

"We have some good ground surveillance people out here," Woolsey said. "We'd be very happy to provide you some assistance."

"Thank you, no," Freeh replied. "I'm confident we can handle whatever has to be done."

On Monday, September 13, the CIA finally allowed the G's access to its grounds.

That same afternoon, Les Wiser decided to put his entire FBI career on the line.

11

All Sunday evening at home and driving to the field office on Monday morning, Wiser had debated the pros and cons.

‎ ⹁ He made up epigrams. Sometimes, he told himself, it was easier to get forgiveness than to get permission.

More surveillance wasn't the answer. But he just couldn't sit still. After "Black Thursday," morale on the Nightmover squad was not the highest.

Wiser wanted to resume the trash cover. Bear Bryant, his boss, the man who had put him in charge of the squad, had called it off because of the Kessler book. But that didn't appear to be applicable anymore. The question Wiser wrestled with was whether the Bear had called it off permanently. You could argue—couldn't you?—that it was only a suspension. Wiser decided that he didn't want to chance finding out. Bryant had been leery of trash covers in the first place.

Wiser confided only in Mike Anderson.

"We are in a retreat," he said to Anderson. "The time to attack is now. Isn't that right?"

"Sure, I suppose. What are you getting to?"

"Let's attack," Wiser said. "Let's do the trash cover again."

"What about Bear? Is he going along with it?"

"I don't want him to know about it. I'm not sure what he'd say. Why burden him? It's my ass."

Wiser waited. Mike Anderson was a solid guy. If Anderson had said he was nuts even to think about it, Wiser was prepared to drop the whole idea. But Anderson didn't. After a moment, he smiled at the audacity of it. "Faint heart never won fair lady," he said.

Only Wiser and Anderson knew that Bryant had not authorized the trash cover. Wiser didn't want official wrath to fall on anyone else's head, especially the G's, if there was a mishap.

Wiser personally called J. R. Heard. "Go for it."

"Great, man," Heard replied. "Just great!"

A minute before two A.M. on Wednesday, September 15, the black van eased toward the container in front of Rick's house. Agents Mitchell and Spry, as usual, trailed behind.

As the van was about to stop, car headlights were spotted coming up North Randolph, and John "Hooker" Powers had to go around the block for a second pass. It was the first time that had occurred. The earlier trash covers had gone without interruption.

"It's a good sign," "Hooker" whispered to J.R. "The other times were too easy. We're going to get something." Then "Hooker" said, "Rub my head twice for luck. Believe me, it never fails."

The container was rushed to "Hill Street." G's from the special response teams were lined up at the tables to go through the contents. Mike Mitchell was on hand in case any financial papers showed up. Spry stood by.

During an earlier trash cover, J.R. and "Hooker"

had told Spry about a practical joke they had played on agents during a dead drop cover. It was obvious that it wasn't going to come off. So a couple of the G's put a film canister in a milk carton in the suspected drop with a little note in Russian. The next thing they heard was excited radio chatter. "Hey, we've got something over here. We really need to look at this."

And now, in the early morning hours of September 15, one of the G's, Jeff Scerna—"Old Man"—could hardly believe his eyes. He'd found a tiny piece of torn yellow paper, so small that he'd almost missed it. But somehow he had spotted writing on it in hand-printed capital letters. There were two words: "MEET AT."

"Oh, my God, what's this? Come look at this," he gasped to J.R. "I think I've got the big one."

"Keep going," Heard exclaimed when he saw what it was. "Everybody! Look for yellow paper!"

Dell Spry turned to "Hooker." "Listen," he said, "we don't have time for any more jokes. Get back to work."

"Hooker" was so worked up that his throat constricted. Finally, he got the words out. "It's . . . it's not a joke."

Then "Celtic"—Jeff Thompson—discovered another scrap of yellow paper that also had the word "MEET" written on it.

About half of the trash already had been bagged to return in Rick's container. All the bags were opened again.

"Come on," J.R. urged. "There's got to be more of them." The allotted time was running out.

In all, six little pieces of paper were finally retrieved. One was missing and never found. "Stinger"—Todd Healey—put them together one by one. Everyone crowded around. The message, on a two-inch-by-two-inch yellow Post-it, was a draft ver-

sion of one Rick stuck to a package of documents that
he had dropped off on "Black Thursday."

It read:

> I AM READY TO MEET
> AT B ON 1 OCT.
> I CANNOT READ
> NORTH 13-19 SEPT.
> IF YOU <u>WILL</u>
> <u>MEET</u> AT B ON 1 OCT.
> PLS SIGNAL NORTH W [missing]
> OF 20 SEPT TO CONFI [missing]
> <u>NO</u> MESSAGE AT PIPE.
> IF YOU <u>CANNOT</u> MEET
> 1 OCT, SIGNAL NORTH AFTER
> 27 SEPT WITH MESSAGE AT PIPE.

It was an electrifying moment, the breakthrough
that Nightmover had sought for so long, the first
tangible evidence that Rick Ames was spying for the
Russians.

In analyzing the Post-it, Jim Milburn said that "B"
obviously referred to an upcoming meeting that Rick
was scheduled to have in Bogotá with his handler.
"NORTH" must be the signal site that the Russians
used to alert Rick, probably, as the G's suspected,
somewhere along the Military Road route he took to
Langley when he wasn't taking Paul to school.
"PIPE" had to be its companion dead drop. And Rick
was notifying his masters that he would not be in
Washington between September 13 and 19 to get confirmation of the Bogotá meeting. As Nightmover already was aware, he'd be on a CIA mission to Turkey
and the former Soviet Republic of Georgia to attend a
counternarcotics conference.

The torn Post-it was put back together and photographed. While Dell Spry waited for the negative to be

developed, Rick's container was rushed back to North Randolph. It was now nearly four A.M.

There was jubilation at the "Hill Street" site. J.R. cried, "Unbelievable! Fucking unbelievable!"

"I told you," John Powers told him. "All you had to do was rub my head twice. Piece of cake."

Les Wiser was asleep when Spry phoned him at five A.M. "You need to come to the office right now."

"What's going on?"

"Just come in."

It was six o'clock by the time Wiser arrived from his home in Maryland.

Spry, exhausted, had left. But Mike Anderson, who was always the first one in the office in the morning, was there. "We hit the mother lode," Anderson said. Then he showed Wiser a black-and-white photograph of the Post-it message. They ended up hugging one another.

They waited for Bear Bryant to arrive. Anderson handed him the photograph.

"What's this?" Bryant asked. "Hell, I haven't even had my coffee yet."

"Read it, boss," Wiser said, grinning.

"I'll be goddamned," Bryant said. "When did you get this?"

"Last night."

"A trash cover?"

"Yes, sir."

"I'm glad you didn't ask me. I would have said no way. You and your damn trash covers."

"I guess," said Wiser, "I was a little insubordinate."

"Well," Bear Bryant said, "I'll say one thing. This is the nicest bit of insubordination I've ever had." He turned to Mike Anderson. "You were in on this, too?"

"Bear," Anderson said, "the G's deserve all the credit. They did a fantastic job."

Afterward, Wiser exulted, "How about that! In one week, from the outhouse to the penthouse!"

Rick returned from the narcotics conference on September 18. He was greeted by Rosario with the news that in the steady rain that had fallen during his absence, the basement was flooded. Would he please do something about it. It was not delivered as a question.

The next day he was overheard telling Rosario that he had made a reservation on American Airlines to fly to Bogotá via Miami on September 29, to return October 4.

Les Wiser wanted to beat Rick to Bogotá. Get there ahead of him and set up a surveillance. The goal had always been to catch Rick with a Russian handler. And even if they couldn't arrest him in a foreign country, maybe they could photograph him, say, meeting with someone, photograph him passing a package or getting into a car with Russian diplomatic plates. There was some resistance from headquarters. Bogotá would be difficult to operate in, and it wasn't the safest place in the world for FBI agents. But he finally got his way.

Since there weren't going to be any G's available to tail Rick in Bogotá, Wiser intended to use a "picket" surveillance—agents stationed in specific locations that Rick might go by for his rendezvous with his handler. The problem, in a city the size of Bogotá, was where the rendezvous would take place. Jim Milburn thought he had the answer. His files showed that the Russians had used Bogotá for meetings. Their favorite place for them was the Unicentro, a huge enclosed mall on the north side of the city—in a corridor that led to bowling alleys. It looked good to Wiser. The Unicentro was not far from either the Russian embassy or the apartment Rick would be staying in, the one he had bought for Rosario and his mother-in-law, Cecilia.

Wiser flew down with Mike Donner and four Hispanic agents he had borrowed temporarily from other squads at the field office. In Bogotá, on the morning of October 1, he was preparing to go to the airport to observe Rick's arrival when he got a call from Mike Anderson in Washington.

"It's off," Anderson said. "Come on home."

What had happened was that in his Post-it, Rick had written that if there were any changes in plans regarding the Bogotá trip, he was to be notified after September 27. And on the morning of September 29, on his way to work at Langley, with Wiser in Bogotá, he'd seen a white chalk mark at signal site "North," the telephone pole that the KGB—now the SVRR—used on Military Road. That afternoon he'd driven to Wheaton Regional Park, to dead drop "Pipe," to retrieve a message. It said that the Bogotá date had been changed. Further instructions would be left for him in "Pipe" on October 3.

He'd phoned Rosario from Langley. "Is your day going okay?"

"As well as can be expected. I'm so tired."

"Well, take it easy. By the way, there's news. No travel."

"Oh?"

"So you should, I guess you should give Ceci a call and tell her, you know, that, ah, that they, I mean, my visit was canceled."

"When will you go?"

"I'll know in a couple of days."

"Does that mean you have to retrieve something again?"

"Yeah, uh-huh."

On Sunday morning, October 3, at "Pipe," there was an envelope wrapped in plastic in the culvert.

Rick read the handwritten message at Dunkin' Donuts. It said: "Are ready to meet at a city well known
to you on 1 Nov. Alt dates are 2,7,8 Nov." If that
suited Rick, he was to leave a mark before October 17
at signal site "Smile," the other mailbox at 37th and
R Streets.

The message also advised that cash would be ready
for him and ended "Best regards."

On his cellular phone, he called Rosario. "All is
well. I'm bringing home doughnuts for breakfast."

But Rosario had far more than breakfast on her
mind.

"Financially, too?" she asked.

"Ah, yeah. Wait till I get there."

On October 6, during another trash cover, an odd item
was discovered. At first, nobody at "Hill Street"
could figure out what it was. It looked like an old reel-
to-reel audiotape with the reels missing. On closer
examination, it turned out to be a ribbon of some
sort. And you could see that the ribbon had reverse
indentations of letters on it. But it was clearly too big
to be a typewriter ribbon. Then one of the G's said,
"I think it's from one of those computer printers that's
gone out of style."

J. R. Heard put it in a plastic bag and sent it over
to the field office. In anticipation of gathering more
evidence in the wake of the Post-it discovery, Wiser
had added a new agent named John Hosinski to Nightmover. Unlike the others, Hosinski came from a criminal squad and had invaluable experience in the proper
handling of evidence. At first, he was reluctant to join
up. He was happy working criminal homicides on a
squad where he was number two. He didn't know
Wiser well, and Wiser had said he couldn't tell Hosinski what was involved until he agreed to come on
board. But Rudy Guerin and Mike Donner convinced

him it was worthwhile. Guerin and Donner were pals of Hosinski's. They'd gotten to know each other playing in the same softball league.

And now, Wiser gave Hosinski the computer ribbon or whatever it was. Maybe the FBI lab could do something with it.

Right then, however, everyone on Nightmover was focusing on a momentous turn in the investigation. The search-and-seizure authorization signed by Attorney General Reno was about to be exercised. And to install bugs.

Rick and Rosario were to attend a wedding in Florida on Saturday, October 9. The only question was whether Paul would be with them. He was. Rick's sister, Nancy, was going to be out of town herself and unavailable for baby-sitting. The house at 2512 North Randolph Street would be vacant from Friday night until Sunday night.

At 1:45 A.M. that Saturday a van came to a stop in front of Rick's house. Technicians brought up from Quantico came out, dressed in black. They went through an unlocked latch gate of a wooden fence extending from the left side of the house as you faced it from the street. The G's had already ascertained that Rick, unlike many of his neighbors, did not have an alarm system. At that end of the house, a stairwell led to a basement door. It was a perfect out-of-sight spot to gain entry, to "make a key."

Picking a lock was a hit-or-miss operation. To make a key, though, was a relatively simple procedure. You inserted a heated, duplicate blank key that matched the make of lock, worked it back and forth for a few minutes until you established where the pins were. Then you filed down the pin marks until the key worked.

But there was an immediate hitch. Rick had

snapped off a key in the lock and had never done anything about it.

This forced the techs to move up to a side kitchen door that would be visible from the neighboring house and the street. Other agents were waiting in cars around the corner. It seemed like an eternity. "Come on, guys," Rudy Guerin kept whispering. In fact, only twenty minutes elapsed before the kitchen door was opened.

The first agent inside, lugging his equipment, was a computer expert named Tom Murray. He went directly to Rick's den to start trying to download what was in his computer. It was a laptop, which meant it couldn't be bugged. To bug a computer, you had to have a continuous power source. Whatever was in it had to be retrieved then and there. Right off, Murray saw that there were protective code words he would have to hack through.

All the shades in the house were drawn. The G's had reported that the previous Thursday a cleaning service was in, vacuuming the rugs. Fortunately, it hadn't rained, which would have invited muddy footprints. Even so, Mike Mitchell and Rudy Guerin decided to remove their shoes in the kitchen. Other agents did the same as they searched through the house.

The Quantico technicians began placing miniature microphones. A camera was set up in a windowless downstairs bathroom to photograph documents. Upstairs, using pencil flashlights, Guerin and Mitchell were finding plenty of them.

In Rosario's study, Mitchell discovered a Riggs Bank register, which was still actively showing deposits. In drawers in the master bedroom were Rick's Credit Suisse account numbers and copies of wire transfers. There also was a Banco International de Colombia account in the name of Cecilia Dupuy de

Casas. One hundred and eleven thousand dollars had been transferred to it from the Credit Suisse account in her name in Zurich. Multiple wire transfers to the Dominion Bank of Virginia were funneled through Citibank in New York. Seventy-five thousand dollars had gone to Morgan Stanley & Company, also in New York, for a money market investment in Pierpont Funds.

And in a top chest drawer, Rudy Guerin unearthed a big-ticket item, the instructions that Rick had received on October 3 for the alternative dates for a November meeting in Bogotá. They had been written on a classified advertisement from the *Washington Times*.

Guerin and Mitchell went downstairs to Rick's den. There was a closet on the far side of it that they wanted to get into. But with Tom Murray's equipment and wires running all over, it was too tight a squeeze. Besides Rick's laptop, a Toshiba, there was a Macintosh computer. It didn't appear to be in use, but Murray was attempting to find out what might also be stored in it. And time was running out. The outside limit for the search to end was five A.M. It was now five minutes to five. Agents stationed on the perimeter of the property reported not a peep from the neighbors. It was not a moment to push their luck.

All Saturday and Sunday, Tom Murray went through the disks he had brought back. Rick turned out to be the ultimate pack rat. Among the material recovered was a nine-page tasking list that Rick had gotten from "Vlad" before leaving Rome in 1989. Also in the computer were his signal sites and dead drops for 1993. Signal site "Rose" was confirmed to be the mailbox at the corner of Garfield Road and Garfield Terrace, and Nightmover now knew where "Smile" was. "Smile" would be the confirmation signal for his November meeting in Bogotá.

Data in the computer also showed that Jim Milburn was correct. The meeting, just as he'd predicted, was to be at the Unicentro mall.

In the euphoria after the successful break-in, the computer ribbon from the October 6 trash cover was overlooked. "What happened to it?" J. R. Heard asked Wiser.

It was still sitting in the field office. The FBI lab had said it was too busy, and since Nightmover remained ultrasecret, whoever made the call was unable to invoke high priority.

John Hosinski took a look at the reverse typeface on the ribbon. "I've got an idea," he said. He disappeared and returned with two plastic spools and attached each end of the ribbon to them. Then he went into a secretary's office and borrowed a small wall mirror she had.

After Tom Murray and Mike Mitchell had rewound the ribbon by hand and started to unspool it again, Hosinski sat on a desk holding the mirror under it, reading out loud what was on the ribbon as seen in the mirror. Wiser had the Nightmover secretary, Linda Williams, take it all down in shorthand.

Surveying the scene, Wiser couldn't help being overcome with laughter. "Boy," he said, "the high-tech FBI in action! Can you imagine what this scene would be like if they did a movie? This ribbon would be whipped off to the lab. Guys would be running around in white coats. Reels would spin. Lights would go up all over the place. And presto! It all would come up on a computer screen in seconds."

Everyone broke up.

"Okay," Wiser said. "Let's get serious."

It was laborious going. The agents kept trading places, one reading from the mirror, the other two spooling.

The words on the ribbon were stunning.

In one communication to Moscow in late August 1992, after his interview by the Playactor team at Langley, Rick had addressed "My dear friends." He wrote: "All is well with me and I have recovered somewhat from my earlier period of pessimism and anxiety. My security situation is unchanged—that is to say, I have no indications of any problems." The next sentence was, "My family is well and my wife has accomodated [sic] herself to understanding what I am doing, in a very supportive way."

It would never be clear exactly what Rosario had accommodated herself to—Rick's spying for the Russians or the fact that he had overcome his own temporary anxiety about it.

But far and away the most significant message was the last one on the ribbon. When the KGB was broken up by Boris Yeltsin, it was divided into two parts, the SVRR for foreign intelligence and the MBRF for domestic security. During the Russian part of his counternarcotics conference, the MBRF certainly had been aware of Rick's presence.

And as Rick smugly noted to Moscow Center, "You have probably heard a bit about me by this time from your (and now my) colleagues in the MBRF."

It was the first physical evidence that directly linked him to Russia's spy network.

The microphones that were installed on North Randolph Street could not have performed better. And there wasn't the slightest indication that Rick or Rosario had noticed anything amiss in the house.

At the command post at the Washington Field Office, agents Julie Johnson and Mike Degnan listened.

On Tuesday, October 12, two days after their return from the Florida wedding, Rick was saying during dinner that he'd have to take cash from his closet to make a deposit. Some bills had to be taken care of. And then he said, "The other thing I have to do is take off early tomorrow to put a signal down."

"You have to what?"

"They would like confirmation that I'm coming."

Rosario wanted to know if Rick was supposed to load another dead drop so soon.

"No. Uh-uh. Just mark the signal."

"Why didn't you do it today, for God's sake? Why wait till the morning?"

"I should have, I suppose, except it was raining like crazy. . . . Before the fourteenth is all they said."

"Well, honey," she said in a condescending tone, "I hope you didn't screw up. . . . All you have to do is a mark?"

"Yeah. Don't worry."

By then Paul had ended his ill-fated attendance at the Burgundy Farms school and was back at Marymount, where Rick would drop him off on the way to Langley. Rosario was annoyed that she'd have to take Paul to Marymount. "Do you have time to go there and come back?" she said.

No problem, Rick said. He'd leave no later than six-thirty. Traffic would be light. It wouldn't take him more than fifteen minutes, he assured her.

"Oh, that early. Oh, okay."

"I'll just go and do it," he said, "And bang! I'm back here."

Rick was as good as his word. He left at 6:22 A.M. and returned at 6:44. At 7:00 A.M. on October 13, a chalk mark on the "Smile" mailbox was photographed by the G's. Later that morning, the mark had been erased.

At home, on the evening of October 25, after Rick had rebooked his flight to Bogotá, Rosario was at him again, reminding him that when he was overseas for the counternarcotics conference, he had told her that several people on his flight had lost their luggage.

"That worries me a lot," she said. "It's happening more and more on airplanes these days. I hear about it all the time, and you know exactly what I mean. You cannot afford to lose a suitcase with what you're carrying, and so perhaps you should use a carry-on for it."

"I am going to use a carry-on."

"But you've been putting the stuff in a suitcase, right?"

"Sometimes, yeah. But I think I'm going to use the carry-on."

"You are going to have to be a little more imaginative about this," Rosario insisted. "You always have this envelope with this big hunk of stuff. I mean, *really!* You have to be more careful."

Once more, Wiser would lead a team to Bogotá.

As incriminating as the evidence was that had been assembled so far, it remained circumstantial.

Rick had yet to be seen with a Russian intelligence officer. He had yet to be caught in the act of handing over classified material. And the documents he had passed on were unavailable. They were all in Moscow.

Represented by top-flight legal talent, Rick could put up quite a fight. Even the admissibility of a lot of the evidence in hand would be the subject of bitter court battles.

There was a thin line between the authorization to gather intelligence on national security grounds and the evidentiary standards required for a criminal prosecution.

As a former prosecutor and federal judge, Louis Freeh was especially sensitive to this. He warned that a "good faith" Chinese wall must be maintained between the Nightmover intelligence-gathering investigation as it now stood and an eventual criminal prosecution by the Justice Department.

"Fruit from a poisoned tree" could become an issue. And he was right.

12

On October 28, two days before Rick was to depart for Bogotá, Rosario asked him if the trip was still on. There hadn't been another postponement, had there?

"No, it's all set."

Well, she said, she had better phone her mother that he was really coming this time. He still intended to stay with Cecilia, didn't he?

"Sure. Where else?"

She said that she thought he had mentioned something about a hotel. And then she asked Rick if he could give her mother five thousand dollars. Perhaps that would keep her quiet for a while. And, "You know, Pablo [Rosario's brother] needs money for a car. Can you lend him eight hundred dollars?"

"I guess so."

"That's all it is with them. Money, money. That reminds me. The other thing we have to do is, if you get the money, and you think it might be advisable, I would, what I would do, would be to leave [the five thousand dollars for Cecilia] in cash. Although it's a big amount of cash to leave, but I guess it's better. You get the money in dollars, right?"

"Right."

"I get so worried. I don't want you to bring back anything that will make them want to look in your luggage."

Rick assured her that nobody was going to mistake him for a dope dealer. And besides, no one looked for money coming in from Colombia. It was the other way around.

On Saturday night, October 30, Rick called from Bogotá.

"I'm here. I made it safely."

"How was the trip?"

"Fine, fine. The only thing was they lost my garment bag." He had debated about telling her, but he realized that if he didn't, her mother would.

"They *what!*"

"The airline lost it. They said a bunch of bags got delayed and didn't make the flight in the Miami airport."

"Oh, my God, I am very, very nervous."

"I know."

"I know you don't give a shit about the suitcase. But, I mean—okay, *fine!*"

"The suitcase will turn up."

"Okay, okay."

"I'm sure it will."

"I'm just hoping you hadn't decided to pack your stuff in it. And you didn't have anything, uh . . ."

"What?"

"You didn't have anything that shouldn't have been in that bag?"

"No, honey."

"So what are you going to do?"

"Tomorrow, I'll do a little shopping. And then on Monday night, I'll be at the Unicentro for a meeting. I'll probably be out for a while."

Early in the evening, November 1, Les Wiser had agents covering every entrance to the Unicentro mall. Rain was pouring down. It was All Saints Day, a holiday in Colombia, and the mall was teeming with people.

Inside, an agent was stationed at the small concourse that led to the bowling alleys. He had a videocamera concealed in an attaché case.

At a quarter to seven, Rick arrived at the mall. Wiser could see the telltale bulge under his raincoat where the documents he was carrying must have been. Rick walked toward the bowling alleys. He stopped, waited, and looked around. He walked back toward the main part of the mall and wandered around some more before returning to the alleys. Then he left the mall, the bulge under his coat still visible. He'd been there for approximately thirty minutes.

Wiser was dumbfounded.

What was going on? Was the Unicentro only the initial contact point for a meeting that would be held elsewhere? Had there been a brush pass during which someone had slipped Rick a note containing further instructions about where to go next? With the mall so crowded, it was hard to tell.

Wiser reviewed the videotape, trying to spot something. But there weren't any answers.

During the October 9 break-in on North Randolph Street, a Bogotá hotel receipt as well as two from restaurants were discovered. Wiser sent agents to these locations in case Rick showed up. It was a wild shot. He wasn't seen again.

That same evening, in the Nightmover command post at the Washington Field Office, Julie Johnson listened as Rosario placed a call to her mother.

"Oh, Rosa, do you want to speak to Rick?"

"Rick? He's there?"

"Yes. Hold on. I'll get him."

"Hi, how are you?" Rick said. His voice was somewhat slurred.

"What's up? Why are you there?"

"It's nothing, nothing. I had, you know, a short meeting this evening."

"Oh."

"Yeah. And I came back and [a friend of Cecilia's] was here and so we had a good time."

"Did you really meet?" Rosario pressed him.

"Uh-huh."

"When did you get back?"

In the command post, Johnson heard Rick asking, "When did I get back?"

Then he told Rosario, "Nine-thirty."

"What's wrong with you? Why do you have to ask my mother when you got back? Don't be an asshole. Have you been drinking?"

"No, honest, honey. Not a drop. Maybe some of Ceci's rum, but that's it."

"Well, the only reason I was upset was because I thought it had all been for nothing and that, you know, you hadn't gotten the . . . the . . ."

"No, no."

"You're sure?"

"Yeah, believe me. It'll be taken care of tomorrow. All the rest of it, you know."

"Okay," Rosario said. "Just be careful. You swear to me that nothing went wrong?"

"Yeah, uh-uh."

"Well, you don't sound too sure. . . . You wouldn't lie to me, would you?"

"No, no. Okay?"

"Okay."

"Good . . . be rest assured. Everything is okay."

"Just be careful tomorrow," Rosario said.

Julie Johnson reached Wiser at his hotel. She spoke guardedly. But what she relayed confirmed his worst fears. It seemed that Unicentro had been a contact meeting. According to Rick, the real meeting, with the documents being passed, would take place the next night at some other location in Bogotá. And where that would be, Rick hadn't given a clue.

Wiser told her that he and the other agents would be flying out in the morning. It'd be pointless to remain in Bogotá. It was another strike three.

What Les Wiser did not know, could not have known, was that Rick, afraid of Rosario's temper, had been lying to her on the phone.

He had gotten the wrong time for the Unicentro meeting on November 1. In Rick's scribbled notes to himself, he had misread "18 hours" [six P.M.] for "19 hours." He had discovered his error only in studying his notes again before downing some Scotches in a bar after he'd left the mall. And he wasn't that concerned. His instructions were to repeat the procedure the following night, same place, if there was some problem.

So on the evening of November 2, he hooked up with "Andrei" by the Unicentro bowling alleys. Rick got into a car and went to the Russian embassy. There he gave "Andrei" the documents he had brought—actually floppy disks in a computer case—and enjoyed some celebratory vodkas.

Rick apologized for the mix-up the previous night. That, said "Andrei," was why there always were fall-back positions. He handed Rick $130,000, this time, for the first time, in crisp new hundred-dollar bills. There was nothing to worry about, "Andrei" said. The cash was from U.S. foreign-aid accounts that Moscow had access to.

The best news of all from "Andrei" was that

despite all the talk of a new era between Russia and the United States, another $1,900,000 had been set aside for Rick.

At the field office, Les Wiser had to listen to Rosario ask, "How was the flight back? Was there any trouble? Everything with the bags was okay?"

"Yeah. It was all normal."

He had left five thousand dollars with Cecilia, he said.

He brought back one hundred and twenty-five thousand dollars in five tightly wrapped packets. He had to deposit some of the cash immediately. They were running short. But guess what? "They're holding—they're holding a million nine hundred thousand," he said.

"So when do you have to go back?" she said. "In a year or what?"

"Yeah, well, maybe not to Bogotá. Either Caracas or Quito, you know, in Ecuador. How do you say it, anyway? Quit-tow? Kee-tow?"

"Why those places? Well, at least it's not Lima. Have you been reading what's going on there? I mean, you could get murdered in Lima. I mean, I'd rather go to Bogotá anytime, even with the drug cartels, than go to Lima."

"Bogotá's getting too unstable, they said."

"Did you give Pablo the money for his car?"

Bear Bryant, meanwhile, got the surprise of his FBI career. The first time he had ever met Louis Freeh was the day Freeh was sworn in as director.

As Freeh was drastically reorganizing the bureau, especially at headquarters, the conventional wisdom was that if he hadn't known you when he was an agent or a prosecutor, you'd never make his inner circle.

But the Ames investigation had made Freeh especially conscious of Division 5, then officially called the intelligence division, although its mandate was really counterintelligence. For Freeh, that symbolized to a large degree what he found lacking in the division. It seemed to him that the CIA culture of collecting intelligence for its own sake had wormed its way into Division 5's thinking. That was fine as far as it went, but the FBI ought to have a better espionage capability. The thrust should be to get out there and make cases—"lock people up."

He decided to rename Division 5 the national security division. He wanted more aggressiveness, against spies and the new domestic threat of foreign terrorism. The more he saw of Bear Bryant during Nightmover, the better he liked him. And Bryant had come out of a background tangling with big-time organized crime. It was just the combination Freeh was searching for.

There was something else as well. Right after he became director, Freeh made a habit of inspecting at least weekly one of the FBI's fifty-six field offices. In the past, whenever a director did this, it was tantamount to a royal visit. But Freeh did it differently. After meeting with office supervisors, he spent most of his time with street agents, squad leaders, and even secretaries to get a feel, as he put it, that the "right ingredients were in place in that particular office." As a result, he had already removed two special agents in charge. And now he was about to make a different kind of change. In visiting the Washington Field Office, Freeh had rarely heard the accolades that were accorded Bryant.

In early November, Bryant met with Freeh and Fred Thomas, the chief of Washington metropolitan police, to implement plans for a new program to combat street crime in the District of Columbia.

As they were coming down the steps at police

headquarters, Freeh turned to Bryant and said, "How would you like to be an assistant director?"

"Of what?"

"Division Five."

Bryant tried to hide his glee. "I'd want to bring John Lewis over with me."

"You can have anyone you want," Freeh said. Then he said, "What about Ames? Shouldn't we be wrapping him up?"

"I agree. But Wiser thinks he may make another drop. Wiser's scrupulous. That's why I picked him. He wants a 'beyond reasonable doubt' case. Ames isn't going anywhere. We have him covered like a blanket, and Wiser says he hasn't shown any sign he knows we're on to him. I vote we give Les a little more time."

But all December, Rick didn't make a move.

Wiser decided to give Julie Johnson and Mike Degnan a Christmas break from their monitoring chores in the command post. He, Mike Donner, John Hosinski, and Rudy Guerin volunteered to pull shifts.

For Guerin, it was the low point of his FBI career. "Here it was, Christmas Eve," he remembered. "My wife and my kids are in Oklahoma at her folks' place. And there I was listening to this son of a bitch, his harridan wife, and their screaming brat."

13

In early January 1994, the FBI's investigation of Rick Ames took a twist so bizarre that it continues to beggar belief.

Unless an actual felony is being observed, the bureau cannot make an arrest in an espionage case without the approval of the internal security section of the Justice Department's criminal division. For more than fifteen years, the section had been under the able leadership of a career department attorney, John L. Martin. During that period, Martin had been in the middle of some bruising intragovernment battles. If it wasn't the intelligence community frantic to bury mistakes by trying to stop a prosecution, it was the FBI yelling that Martin was going overboard on his insistence that a prosecution be denied because it rested on shaky constitutional grounds. And not once had a successful prosecution he had authorized ever been reversed because of illegal procedures.

But Martin had never confronted a situation like the one he was now facing. His own Justice Department superiors were refusing to permit even the prepa-

ration of a draft complaint and arrest warrant against
Rosario.

Les Wiser had spent days at internal security pres-
enting the evidence that the Nightmover squad had so
painstakingly gathered. He had been complimented
on how well the case against the Ameses had been
put together.

"*Why?* What's the reason?" Wiser asked after he
was informed of what was happening.

He was told that the Justice Department's criminal
division—under assistant attorney general Jo Ann
Harris—felt that it would be too embarrassing for the
department if both parents were locked up. Their son,
Paul, would have no custodian. The media would have
a field day.

When Wiser reported this to Bear Bryant, the
Bear, usually not at a loss for words, was rendered
speechless.

Louis Freeh hit the ceiling.

Still, the ultimate call remained with the Justice
Department. Finally, with the FBI as a sort of baleful
Greek chorus, Martin won the day. In retrospect it
was clear that if Martin hadn't, the investigation could
have had an entirely different outcome.

When Christmas, and then January, came and went
without a drop, Wiser was ready to give up hope for
one in the immediate future.

In mid-January, near panic swept the field office
command post. "Oh, my God," Rosario was saying in
a call to Rick, "I think we're being bugged."

"What are you talking about?"

"There's this wire in the garage. It's a white wire
and it's hanging down and I've never seen it before."

"Take it easy. That white wire's from the water
heater. When the workmen were in, they never re-
strung it right. It's always been there."

"Are you sure, Rick? You're sure?"

"Yes, honey," he said. "But good work. That was good of you to notice."

Now time was running out for Wiser. Rick was scheduled to leave Washington on February 22 for Moscow to attend a counternarcotics conference. At the behest of the FBI, the CIA had postponed the trip twice. One time, Rick was told that the CIA director, James Woolsey, had to brief President Clinton on current conditions in Russia. "You're our man on narcotics. We need you to prepare a paper for him." Yet another delay would be asking for trouble.

Then Wiser got hints that there would be a drop after all. The second week in February, Rosario said to Rick, "Don't you have something to put down?"

"I'm not sure. I have to check."

She asked again, "Did you make the signal?"

"No, not yet."

When nothing more happened, Wiser began to think that instead of utilizing a dead drop in Washington, Rick was planning to bring CIA operational secrets with him to Moscow.

In a meeting with Bear Bryant, Louis Freeh said that obviously Ames could not be allowed to make the trip. The specter of Edward Lee Howard still haunted headquarters.

Perhaps Rick had been waiting for just this opportunity to take off. And you couldn't count on him being totally oblivious of what was happening around him. Of course, it would be marvelous to catch him in a drop—and get his Russian contact to boot. "But I think we have enough evidence," Freeh said. "As it stands, we have a very convictable case. And based on what's been picked up in his trash, there's probably more evidence in his house."

The original thought was to arrest Rick on his way to the airport on February 22 in case he was carrying highly classified documents. That idea was discarded. It would be too last minute, leaving no margin for unforeseen error.

In planning the arrests, Les Wiser decided that they should take place in the jurisdiction of the Eastern District of Virginia, on the other side of the Potomac, so that if there were a trial, it would be at the courthouse in Alexandria. Wiser had worked well with the U.S. attorney's office there. Besides, the hard fact was that judges and juries in the eastern district were traditionally more friendly to federal law enforcement than those in the District of Columbia.

Rick and Rosario would be transported to an FBI facility at Tysons Corner. To soften up Rick especially, he'd be brought to a room that had been made up to look like a command post, with surveillance blowups of him on the walls; other photos of the signal sites and dead drops he had used; a huge map of Bogotá with the Unicentro mall circled in red; a photograph of the Russian embassy in Rome; another of his initial Soviet contact, the diplomat, Sergei Chuvakhin; and enlargements of some CIA personnel files relating to him. Phone messages were on a bulletin board: "Les, Please call Rudy." "Les, Anderson must speak to you." A blackboard had the dates of Rick's travel overseas. Empty pizza boxes and coffee cups were strewn about.

Rudy Guerin was to see what he could get out of Rick after he was taken into custody. Wiser chose John Hosinski to question Rosario. He had a low-key style that would be just right. Julie Johnson had been listening to Rosario for months, and she told Wiser and Hosinski that the best approach was not to put Rosario in a corner where she'd get her back up. Rosario, Julie said, was a control freak. Make her feel that somehow she was still in charge. She was a snob. She would respond to what she perceived to be respect. Wiser picked agent Yolanda Larson to be with Hosinski, so Rosario couldn't claim later that she had been badgered by two male ogres. Larson spoke elegant Spanish. She was also eight months pregnant, and that might make Rosario feel less threatened.

But the most important advice that Julie Johnson gave was that Rosario was a survivor. She said that handled deftly, Rosario would instinctively act to save her own skin. She'd sacrifice Rick in an instant if she decided that it was to her advantage. "And even her son," Johnson said. Rosario could be the key, Wiser thought.

Wiser wanted Rick and Rosario to be collared separately, so that they wouldn't have even a minute to confer with one another. Wiser was adamant on one more point. Neither of them was to be apprehended in the presence of five-year-old Paul. "I'm serious about this," Wiser said. "He's just a kid. He doesn't deserve the trauma. He didn't do anything wrong. Too bad his mother and father didn't think about what they were doing to him."

Arrangements had to be made to get him to a child welfare center. Then Julie Johnson had a better idea. Rick's sister, Nancy, didn't live far away. After the arrests, perhaps she should be contacted. In monitoring life in the Ames household, Julie had been privy to several visits the sister had made. She had raised a family of her own, and she and the boy got along quite well. "As a matter of fact, speaking as a mother," Julie said, "I think Paul would be better off with Nancy regardless. The kid's a wreck as it is with all the screaming going on."

The date for the arrests was set for Monday, February 21.

Then someone realized that February 21 was Presidents' Day, a holiday. Rick and Rosario would both be in the house. So would Paul. To complicate things further, Cecilia had arrived from Bogotá to be with Rosario while Rick was in Moscow. Fall-back plans had to be devised.

Bear Bryant asked Freeh if he would like to be in the command post at headquarters.

"No," Freeh said. "It's your case. I'd just be in the way. I'll be home. Call me after it goes down."

14

By seven-thirty A.M., the entire Nightmover squad, except for Mike Degnan, had assembled in a parking lot at a Roy Rogers restaurant near the FBI's Tysons Corner facility. Degnan was at the field office command post to handle the phones and radio traffic. Fifteen additional agents culled from other counterintelligence squads were also present to search Rick's office at Langley, to move into, photograph and search his house, and to provide whatever backup was necessary.

At eight o'clock, the arrest and interview cars departed. Rudy Guerin was with Mike Donner and Dell Spry in Donner's Chevrolet sedan. Behind them were two more cars carrying FBI SWAT teams. Half an hour later, they parked at a Safeway supermarket off Lee Highway, a few blocks south of Rick's neighborhood. They waited.

At nine o'clock, Guerin got out of the car and started walking around in tight little circles. He chatted briefly with the SWAT teams. Jeez, he thought, why hasn't Degnan called? He should have called by now.

It all had been prearranged. To get Rick out of the house on this holiday morning and separate him from Rosario, Degnan was to have the CIA's chief of counternarcotics, Dave Edgers, summon him to Langley.

At nine-thirty, Guerin said to Donner, "Let's call Degnan. Find out what's what." When Donner phoned Degnan, Degnan said, "It's happening. You'll get it on your radio."

They could hear the phone ringing. Then Rosario was answering and Edgers identified himself and said, "Can I speak to Rick, please."

Edgers's breaths were rapid—and nervous. "Stay cool," Rudy whispered.

"Dave?" Rick said.

"Yes. Sorry to bother you. But I've got a cable here regarding the trip. Think you could come in and take a look at it?"

"Sure. I can leave in about fifteen minutes."

Donner and the SWAT teams pulled out.

Rick's route to Langley was to come around a curve on North Randolph Street and turn right on Quebec. Then Quebec intersected with a wide avenue called Nellie Custis Drive, where he would turn left again toward Military Road. The SWAT cars were positioned at the Nellie Custis intersection.

Donner, meanwhile, parked on North Randolph, facing the direction that Rick was coming from. Five minutes later, a G stationed by the house radioed, "He's out of the garage."

They saw the Jaguar rounding the bend. Rick slowed to turn right on Quebec. They could see him lighting a cigarette.

As soon as Rick was on Quebec, Donner moved up behind him. Ahead of Rick, the two SWAT cars were bumper to bumper across Quebec at Nellie Custis. Guerin had been leery of this part of the operation. Suppose Rick panicked, thinking it was a holdup, and tried to run up the sidewalk and across a lawn? Suppose somebody chose that moment to come out of a front door? Suppose Rick had a gun nobody knew about?

But Rick would have no time to really think about anything.

Mike Donner started flashing a red light that sat on his dashboard. He turned on his siren. Rick slowed toward the curb, as if to let Donner pass him. He stopped a few feet short of one of the SWAT cars. Donner came right up to the rear of the Jaguar.

He sprang from his car. Dell Spry came around from the other side, gun in hand. Donner, whose favorite sport was rugby, raced to the driver's side of the Jaguar. Rick, looking bewildered behind his thick glasses, was rolling down his window. A Benson & Hedges cigarette dangled between his lips. Donner reached in and jerked it away. "FBI," Donner said, holding up his badge. "You're under arrest!" Then Donner opened the door and yanked Rick into the street.

"For what?" Rick cried. "For what?"

"For espionage," Donner said. "Put your hands on the roof of your car."

"*What!*" Rick cried again. "This is unbelievable. *Unbelievable!*"

Rudy Guerin had moved back. Since he was the one who had to try to get Rick to talk, he didn't want Rick to associate him directly with what was happening. Guerin glanced at his watch. Amazing! Not more than sixty seconds had elapsed.

Dell Spry patted Rick down. Rick was wearing khaki pants, a dark blue polo shirt, and a leather jacket. All Spry found was a Gucci wallet in his back pocket. Spry ordered Rick to put first one hand and then the other behind his back, and then he handcuffed him.

Spry pushed Rick onto the rear seat of Donner's Chevrolet. Only then did Guerin slide in next to him. Over his radio, Donner said, "We have subject one in custody. We are en route to Tysons Corner." Donner announced the mileage on his odometer. People arrested often claimed that they had been taken off somewhere and beaten up to try to make them confess.

Rick appeared on the verge of hyperventilating. "This is a mistake!" he kept repeating. "This is a terrible mistake!"

"Mr. Ames," Guerin said, "my name is Rudy Guerin. As you've just been told, you are under arrest for espionage."

"Unbelievable! Unbelievable!"

Very softly, Guerin said, "Why is it unbelievable? Can you tell me why?"

All Rick did was roll his head back. "Aaahhh," he muttered, as though in disgust.

"Mr. Ames," Guerin said, "we're going to our resident office at Tysons Corner. We will be in an interview room where you're going to be given an opportunity to cooperate and tell your side of the story. I'm sure you must have one. I also have to tell you that your wife, Rosario, is going to be arrested."

"Oh, God."

"What do you think her reaction's going to be?"

"She'll be terrified."

"Why?" Guerin said.

"Why do you think?" Rick said.

That was as far as Guerin dared venture. He'd been warned repeatedly by the U.S. Attorney's Office in Alexandria that this was not like the Chinese interpreter case, where the suspect was not going to be arrested, where Rudy could use any stratagem he desired. Guerin was going to have to read Ames his rights. And he was not to resort to anything that smacked of prior coercion—using either the wife or the boy as leverage.

Guerin gave it one last shot. "Rick," he now said, "don't tell me you didn't know that this day would come. Don't tell me you didn't think about it. Look, maybe you made a mistake we can straighten out."

Rick did not respond. He was staring straight ahead. Then he tilted his face upward and closed his eyes, as if in self-hypnosis. Guerin heard him mumbling over and over to himself, "Think. Think. Think."

Guerin had this sinking feeling that he wasn't going to get anywhere. Suddenly, he recalled a conversation that Rick had been overheard having with his son.

The two had been playing cops-and-robbers.

Paul had said, "Stick up your hands. You're under arrest."

"Oh, are you a policeman?" Rick had replied.

"Yes. And you're going to jail."

"Well, you didn't even Mirandize me."

"What's that?"

"It means that if you arrest someone, you have to advise him that he has a right to a lawyer."

As they approached Tysons Corner, Guerin said, "It's really your last chance to do yourself some good. You ought to give it some thought."

Donner's radio came on. "Subject number two is in custody and we have secured the house."

"Oh, fuck!" Rick said. His chin dropped to his chest.

John Hosinski and Yolanda Larson had parked in front of 2512 North Randolph. As soon as they learned that Rick had been arrested, Hosinski knocked on the front door. A maid opened it. "We'd like to see Mrs. Ames," he said.

The maid let them in the foyer.

Just then Rosario came down the stairs. She was wearing a beige cashmere turtleneck sweater, a brown skirt with a plaid pattern in it, and a matching vest. She was made up, as if she were ready to go out. She looked inquiringly at them.

"Mrs. Ames," Hosinski said quietly, "I'm with the FBI. This is my associate, Mrs. Larson. Your husband has just been arrested by our agents for conspiracy to commit espionage. You're being arrested on the same charge."

Rosario stared at them. She did not display a flicker of emotion. Finally, she said, "Well, this can't be."

At that moment, Paul appeared.

Hosinski looked at him and then said to Rosario, "Why don't we step out on the porch, so we can explain to you in a little privacy what's happening?"

Outside, he told her, "We know your mother is here. You can talk to your mother. Take as much time as you need within reason. Tell her whatever you wish about why you have to leave. After you've talked to her, speak to your son. We don't care what you tell him. It's up to you. Then we will have to go to our office in Tysons Corner."

Yolanda Larson accompanied Rosario upstairs, where she told Cecilia, still in bed, that something involving her work had arisen and she would be gone for a while. "Please take care of Paul."

Paul seemed intrigued by Hosinski's presence. There was no sign of the tantrums that had been heard from him so often.

After chatting about school, Hosinski asked him if he had a favorite TV show.

"*Power Rangers,*" the boy said.

Upstairs, Larson told Rosario to remove her jewelry and the watch she was wearing. After they all left the house, Hosinski spoke briefly on the walk to Mike

Mitchell, who was to direct other agents in searching the premises. "The mother's upstairs," Hosinski said.

Rosario remained stone faced.

At Tysons Corner, Rick was led into the mock command post. Donner sat him on a chair at a long table and removed his handcuffs. Rick squinted at all the paraphernalia that had been placed on the walls. He started to get up to examine some of the photographs. Donner put a hand on his shoulder. "Stay there," he said.

Guerin sat opposite Rick. "Rick," he said, "before we get going here, I'm going to repeat what we've already told you. You're under arrest for espionage. Your wife is also under arrest. We know what you've been doing and how long you've been doing it. And we know who you've been doing it for. One thing we don't know, and you can help us out, and maybe help yourself, too, is why you've been doing it."

Rick asked if he could have a cigarette.

"No, not right now," Guerin said.

Coffee?

"I'll have somebody get some. But right now I have to advise you of your rights. Here's an advice-of-rights form. Take a couple of minutes to read it. If you understand it and you agree to waive your rights, I want you to sign the form stating such."

Rick picked up the form, glanced at it, and slid it back at Guerin. "I'm not signing anything," he said.

"Can I ask why?"

"Sure. From what I know about the FBI all these years, they usually do a very thorough job in their investigations, and I'm sure you've done a very thorough job with this one. I think I need to speak to an attorney."

"Are you asking for an attorney?"

"I want an attorney."

"Then," said Guerin, "this conversation is over. I can't ask any more questions until you have an attorney present."

All at once, a smug look came over Rick's face. "You can ask anything you want," he said. "I just won't answer."

Guerin left the room and found Mark Hulkower, the assistant U.S. attorney from the eastern district, who would be the lead prosecutor in the case.

"He refused to sign the waiver. He wants a lawyer."

"Okay," Hulkower said. "Lock him up. Who's he want?"

"He didn't say."

When Guerin returned to Rick, he asked what lawyer he wanted. Rick said Bruce Gair, an attorney in Vienna, Virginia. Guerin already knew from the record who he was. He had rented Rick the apartment he and Rosario first lived in after Mexico City. He'd also handled some matters in Rick's divorce from Nancy. Certainly he didn't have the background for a case like this.

"How about my coffee?"

Guerin finally fetched him a cup.

"Where am I going now?"

"To the detention center in Alexandria."

Mike Donner patted him down again. The CIA had cautioned them to make sure Rick didn't have a pill on him. The agency didn't want a suicide. The frame on his glasses should be especially checked in case there was a tiny compartment to secrete a cyanide tablet. But there was no poison.

All Donner found, in Rick's wallet, were nine crisp, new hundred-dollar bills, part of the loot he had received from "Andrei" in Bogotá.

"Can I smoke at the detention center?" Rick asked.

"No," Guerin said. "It's a smoke-free jail."

"Well, how about a cigarette now?"

Guerin thought it over. Somewhere down the line, he might have another crack at Rick. "Okay," he said. "Just one."

Although Rick did not know it, Rosario was already in the building. What bothered Rudy Guerin more than anything was that all this guy wanted to know was whether he could smoke in the detention center.

He hadn't asked a single word about his wife. Or his son.

Remembering Julie Johnson's injunction not to pressure Rosario if possible, John Hosinski waited until she was on the rear seat of the car, sitting next to Yolanda Larson, before she was handcuffed. By now, some neighbors were gawking, wondering what was up.

Larson asked her politely to extend her hands. "I'm sorry, but I have to put these on. It's a matter of procedure."

Hosinski drove. Another agent, who would handle the detention center paperwork, was in front with him. But Hosinski didn't mention anything about jail. He said that they would be going to the FBI's Tysons Corner office. "We'll process you," he said, "and then we can sit down and go over everything with you. You'll be able to call your mother and see how your son is."

Rosario stayed silent.

At Tysons Corner, Hosinski started to bring Rosario into the fake command post, but after a second's reflection, he decided that it wasn't such a good idea and brought her into an interview room. He had Yolanda sit next to Rosario.

It was 11:15 A.M.

Hosinski handed her a copy of the rights waiver form. In Spanish, Larson asked her if she wanted a form in that language. "Oh, you speak very well," Rosario said in English. But no, it wasn't necessary.

As soon as the arrests had been made, Wiser dispatched Julie Johnson to the apartment of Rick's sister, Nancy, and her husband, Hugh Everly.

Everly, a retired army officer, came to the lobby.

After identifying herself, Johnson said, "I have something to tell you, but I'd prefer to tell you with your wife present."

In the apartment, she told them that Rick—and Rosario—had been arrested for espionage. Nancy sagged. Julie helped her to a sofa.

Almost at once, her husband said of Rosario, "That bitch!"

Rick's sister was shaking her head. "Please don't say that. Please calm down. Just calm down until we learn some more."

Clearly, Rick's sister was in shock. But she was holding herself together, just as Johnson thought she would.

"Where are they now, my brother and his wife?"

"I believe they are being questioned at our office in Tysons Corner."

"And Paul? Where's Paul?"

"He's at home. With his grandmother. Actually, I was hoping you would look after him, at least for today, so that we know he's in good hands."

"Of course. I'll go right away. I'll follow you."

At the house, Johnson found Cecilia in near hysterics in the living room. Two Spanish-speaking agents were trying to settle her down. One of them said to Julie, "What's with her?"

Julie Johnson had been listening to Cecilia for more than eight months. "She's a whining, conniving woman," she said. "She can play real stupid when she wants—and smart when she decides that's the way to go."

The moment Paul saw Rick's sister, he shouted an enthusiastic, "Hi!" He seemed oblivious of what had been going on. Then Nancy took Paul and Cecilia home with her.

At Tysons Corner, Rosario signed her waiver of rights. She still looked quite self-possessed.

Treat her as an equal, Julie Johnson had advised. Be sympathetic. Hosinski suggested that she might want to check on Paul.

But on the first ring, an answering machine came on.

Hosinski said that he believed that Cecilia and Paul might be with Rick's sister. They would try a little later.

Hosinski noted that Rosario hadn't inquired about Rick.

She asked if she could go to the rest room. Yolanda Larson escorted her. When she returned, she wanted to know if she could have some coffee. And could she smoke?

"Of course," John Hosinski said.

Make her feel that she's in control.

Hosinski assured her that she could break off the interview whenever she wanted to. If she felt that she needed to consult an attorney, that was fine, too.

Rosario acknowledged that she knew her husband worked for the CIA. She didn't quite understand, however, what his duties were. She denied that she had ever aided anyone in espionage. She was not aware of any relationship Rick had with the Russians or of any espionage-type activities he had engaged in.

She said that she wasn't sure, but she believed that Rick's salary was about sixty thousand dollars a year.

Did she think that this amount was sufficient to support their lifestyle, to allow the purchase of a home like the one they lived in, a car like the one Rick owned?

She said that she knew they had more money available than seemed possible on Rick's salary. But she said that he had been involved in some successful investments with an old friend from Chicago. She said that she was under the impression that this money doubled their annual income.

"Have you ever met this friend?" Hosinski asked.

"No."

Could she identify the friend?

No.

Did she know where the friend now lived?

No.

Did she know how Rick had met him?

No.

"How long has your husband known him?"

"I don't know."

Hosinski did not challenge any of this, that it was rather incredible that all these years could pass without Rosario expressing the slightest interest in Rick's mysterious friend and benefactor. But he could see Rosario for the first time shifting uneasily on her chair.

She wondered if she could check on her son.

Hosinski went out of the room and arranged with the command post to have Rick's sister call in. Rosario spoke to Nancy and then to her mother. Nancy reassured her that Paul was all right.

About an hour had passed.

Rosario volunteered that she didn't question Rick because he handled all the family finances, the paying of bills, filing income tax returns, whatever else had to be done. She acknowledged that there was considerable cash in the house. She assumed it came from the investments.

"We've noticed," Hosinski said, "that your husband has made a lot of deposits in his checking accounts in cash."

She couldn't explain why, she said. She was just a housewife.

Hosinski nodded sympathetically. He got a little more personal. Did Rick provide support for Rosario's mother?

Yes, she replied. Her father was dead and had left no inheritance. Her mother was a schoolteacher in Colombia, which was an ill-paid profession. She guessed that her mother got about $1,200 a month from Rick. She said that Rick had purchased an apartment in the Colombian city of Cartagena that her mother used. She believed that it cost $100,000. She didn't mention the Bogotá apartment. She also said that her mother didn't know that Rick worked for the CIA. The CIA, she said, was not well thought of in many Latin American countries, including Colombia.

At 1:45 P.M., Hosinski offered her lunch. She settled instead for a Coke and a cigarette.

Now that she thought about it, she said, the money for the North Arlington home had come from a Swiss bank account that Rick had. The Jaguar, though, had been paid for partly by a trade-in and partly financed with a term loan. She wasn't sure how her Honda was bought.

Rosario asked if she could speak to Rick's sister once more about Paul. Another phone call was arranged. She asked Nancy if Paul and her mother could stay with her. "Absolutely," Nancy said. "Please don't concern yourself about them."

Hosinski began probing Rosario about Rick's last trip to Bogotá the previous November. She replied that she thought it had been "work related."

Was she aware that he had returned with a large sum of cash?

She said yes and that she was "a little worried" about this. She stated that Rick told her it was from his "Chicago friend."

She asked if she could go to the rest room again.

When she returned, she was twisting some tissue paper in her hands. As she sat down, she continued to work the paper, shredding it.

Then, at ten minutes to three that afternoon, just as Julie Johnson predicted she would, Rosario gave up Rick.

She had not been entirely truthful, she said. "I don't know what to do."

Yolanda Larson leaned over and touched her arm. "Telling the truth will make you feel better, and it will help you in the long run. You have to think of what's best for you and your son."

Rosario looked at Larson. "I want to start telling the truth," she said. "I want to be completely truthful." She confessed that she was aware that Rick had been passing information to the Russians and that he received payments from them for this information.

She said that she had learned this only in the late summer of 1991—or perhaps 1992, she wasn't certain—when she discovered "a strange slip of paper" in a spare wallet of Rick's. She recalled seeing typed "instructions on what to do and how to contact someone." She also recalled the phrase "our embassy."

She said that she thought this was a "very strange message." But when she questioned Rick, he first indicated that it was something he "was working on," leading her to surmise that it might be a "double-agent ploy."

But doubts nagged at her, she said, and a month

later, as she continued to be persistent in questioning him, he finally revealed that he was working with the Russians and "doing it for the money." It was money, he said, to help support her mother and to pay for all the other things they needed.

She said that she believed he had started with the Russians around the time of their marriage. She insisted that she had begged Rick to stop what he was doing.

Rick, she said, had replied that he had told "his people" that at some point he was going to cease his association with them and retire. He also said, according to Rosario, that the Russians had asked him for pictures of herself and their son, but that he had refused to honor this request.

She said that she did not know how many times Rick received money from the Russians. It was her understanding, however, that additional funds were being held for him that he'd get when he finally severed his ties with them.

At 4:00 P.M., Assistant U.S. Attorney Hulkower joined the interview as Rosario continued her story.

At 5:15, the interview was concluded. Rosario told Hulkower that she had been treated well by Hosinski and Larson. "They have been very kind to me," she said.

She was photographed and fingerprinted. At 5:50, she was handcuffed again. Yolanda Larson and another agent drove her to the Alexandria detention center.

She had not once asked about Rick.

That afternoon at 2512 North Randolph, agent Gene McClelland Jr., pressed into service to help search the house, was taking inventory in the master bedroom.

In a closet, there were sixty purses, half of them still in wrapping paper.

Mike Mitchell found women's shoes lined up behind the sliding doors of what once must have been attic crawlspace. After he got to five hundred pairs, he stopped counting. God, he thought, Rosario could really give Imelda Marcos a run for her money.

In other closets, there were dozens upon dozens of ensembles neatly arranged on hangers, many of them with their sales tags on.

But what really got Gene McClelland was what was stacked in some of Rosario's chest drawers. Transfixed, he counted every last one—a hundred and sixty-five unopened boxes of panty hose.

15

On Tuesday morning, February 22, the day Rick Ames had been scheduled to leave for Russia, he and Rosario were arraigned in a federal courtroom jammed with reporters. They were barely able to nod to one another before facing U.S. magistrate Barry Poretz.

Since their assets were frozen, they required court-appointed attorneys. Poretz asked a former U.S. attorney for the eastern district, William Cummings, to represent Rosario.

But it was the court appointment of Rick's lawyer that had Les Wiser groaning inwardly. He was Plato Cacheris, who not only was a peerless defense attorney in Washington, but was held in high esteem by the FBI and the Department of Justice for both his fairness and ferocity in court. The sour joke making the rounds of the Washington Field Office was that the magistrate must be in the pay of the Russians.

Cacheris's normal hourly billings were four hundred dollars. Representing Rick would get him forty dollars an hour for time spent out of court and sixty dollars in it (plus five dollars a day for travel). But he was famous for not turning down a court request like this if the matter wasn't frivolous. And he had just come off a rather lucrative defense of a Saudi Arabian sheikh caught in the BCCI banking scandal and was about to begin a huge international case representing a Volkswagen executive who had been accused by General Motors of stealing trade secrets.

Cacheris also was quick on his feet—in court and in person. When a reporter interviewing him mentioned that he had written articles about Cacheris's professional rivals in Washington, Brendan Sullivan, who had represented Oliver North, and Robert Bennett, who was representing President Clinton against sexual harassment charges, he replied, "I know, and every time you do, people call and ask me if I'm dead."

As Les Wiser feared, client Ames, however currently indigent, would not get short shrift from Cacheris. Before it was over, Cacheris would confer at length with Rick fifty-seven times, in addition to a number of other meetings with a young Cacheris associate, Preston Burton.

The first of these encounters took place at the detention center only hours after Rick's arraignment, on the evening of February 22. Even Rick was impressed. "I was wondering what I would do for a lawyer," he said, "and I get Plato Cacheris!"

But that same evening, Rick negated a key element of a possible trial defense. He told Cacheris that the allegations against him were accurate. He had been supplying the Russians with classified information for a long time—and for money. That meant Cacheris as an officer of the court (although it's not been unknown for other lawyers to wink at this) could not be a party to perjury and put Rick on the witness stand on his own behalf.

What went through the mind of an attorney of his stature at a moment like that?

"Well, of course," he said, "I don't approve of espionage at any time or on any level. But I completely put that out of my head, what Rick did, and viewed it as a legal case which a lawyer had been given the task of defending. And that defense now could not have taken the form of 'I didn't do it.' The defense would have to be that you guys ('you' meaning the U.S. government) have committed some improprieties here and your evidence should not be admitted in court because of these flaws."

The government, Cacheris continued, had to play by the rules. "That's what distinguished us from the very country that Ames was spying for, where they didn't have any rules, where there weren't any rights. He had rights. I did think, during the course of this case, if he had been caught in Russia for espionage, he would have been executed. He certainly would not have had the right to mount a legal challenge that might be sustained by a court. And the part of the system here that I am proud of is the fact that all these rights were protected, even for a guy who committed one of the most heinous crimes of the century—espionage against your own country. He betrayed the CIA. He betrayed the United States. He caused the deaths of people who were working for the American government. I cannot defend that. But I can also say, without any hesitation, that he was entitled to a vigorous defense, and that was what we were prepared to give him."

That first evening at the detention center, when Rick confessed his guilt, what Rick wanted was favorable treatment for Rosario. Neither he nor Cacheris knew—not that it would have made any difference in the end—that Rosario, in an effort to exculpate herself, had already given a statement to the FBI that Rick had been in Moscow's employ.

Almost as though he had anticipated what was now going on, Rick exhibited intimate knowledge about the fate of the spouses of two other spies who were caught and convicted. One was the wife of U.S. Navy warrant officer John A. Walker Jr., who had known for seventeen years that her husband was selling vital intelligence to the Soviet Union. But a bitter Laura Walker, estranged from Walker, escaped punishment because she had turned in her by then ex-husband before anybody knew what he was doing.

The other, more pertinent case, Rick pointed out, was the wife of Jonathan Jay Pollard, a civilian research specialist for the Naval Investigative Service, who passed on hundreds of classified documents to Israel. Clearly, his wife, Anne, had been more than a passive participant, even attempting to dispose of incriminating documents by stuffing them in a suitcase and running off with it once she realized that he was in trouble. But when Pollard, in admitting his crimes, pleaded for mercy for his wife, she ended up serving only three years.

Cacheris said that he did not know what the hold was that Rosario had over Rick. There'd been rumors, speculation, of what it was, at least when their relationship began in Mexico City, but he had never gotten into that. He was Rick's lawyer, not his psychiatrist. It was none of his business. And even if he had probed, he doubted that he would have gotten anywhere. Rick, he said, was a "very private person."

During the next few days, Assistant U.S. Attorney Hulkower let Cacheris and Rick have a look at some of the material that had been unearthed at 2512 North Randolph after his arrest. Along with $7,800 in more crisp hundred-dollar bills from Bogotá, a treasure trove of incriminating paper—messages, travel receipts, notes, Swiss bank transfers, a list of Rick's new signal sites for 1994—were discovered squirreled away on a shelf of the closet in Rick's den—the closet that Rudy Guerin hadn't been able to get into during the October 9 break-in because of all the computer downloading that was going on.

Even Rick was amazed at what he had left lying around. "I guess I got sloppy," he told Cacheris. "After a while, you know, it got so easy that I became careless."

The CIA, meanwhile, was already embarking on a near incoherent campaign of leaking stories essentially aimed at disassociating itself from Rick—trying to explain him away as a stumblebum, an alcoholic underachiever, an unimaginative, plodding nerd who probably couldn't figure out how to get to the post office to mail a letter. Suddenly, colleagues and superiors of Rick's in the CIA were being trotted out, some named, most anonymous, who reeled off one transgression after another that he had committed during a vodka-soaked career, although very little of this had ever appeared in his official agency records.

The truth was that Rick was an excellent debriefer, who wrote incisive analyses on intelligence matters when called upon. His obvious shortcoming was his failure to recruit agents for the CIA when posted overseas. This was partially due to his own nature, his inability to reach out to people. It also was partially because he was quite occupied with working exceedingly well for another employer.

From Moscow, right after his arrest, came an accolade. "He defended our interests," declared the chief of the Russian General Staff.

On March 1, a preliminary hearing on "probable cause" and the continued detention of Rick and Rosario was held before Magistrate Poretz in Alexandria.

Unlike procedures in many state jurisdictions, such as, say, the preliminary hearing in the O. J. Simpson case in California, federal preliminary hearings severely limit the scope of cross-examination, and Plato Cacheris was under no illusion that he would make much headway. And almost every time he attempted to elicit substantive information from Les Wiser, the government's sole "probable cause" witness, Poretz sustained prosecution objections that these were matters reserved for a "discovery" evidentiary hearing before trial.

Still, in hammering at just when the investigation went from an intelligence case involving national security to one that was criminal, Cacheris got Wiser to concede that it was a "hybrid" situation.

He also got from Wiser what he considered a significant admission for trial use—that despite the FBI's "massive" surveillance of Ames, he was never once seen with, or passing documents to, a Soviet or Russian intelligence official.

In meetings with Assistant U.S. Attorney Hulkower, Cacheris got Hulkower to agree that the deaths of any Soviets would not be pursued. Whether they had occurred or not, there was no way of proving in court that they were caused by Ames. Certainly, as matters stood, no Soviet or Russian could be expected to take the stand and testify otherwise.

Cacheris entered a plea of "not guilty" for Rick, as did William Cummings for Rosario.

He was not simply going through the motions. He believed there was a real chance to make a deal, despite the existence of the Classified Intelligence Procedures Act, which drastically curbed a defendant's use of so-called graymail—to force the government in making its case to disclose openly material that it wished to keep secret.

And Cacheris had other leverage. He knew the

CIA was desperate to learn how Rick had pulled off his spying, what he had given to Moscow, how he had obtained his information, what his communication techniques were, and whether he had been working alone or with accomplices. The only person who could come up with the answers was Rick himself.

There were joint meetings with Rick and Rosario. They were awkward and unpleasant. Rosario would rant at Rick. He'd fucked up. He'd gotten her in this mess. How could he have been so stupid? He was responsible for her being in this terrible place.

During these outbursts, he remained silent, staring into space. Tears sometimes would slide down his cheeks.

There was an extensive hearing on Rick's assets, which the government wanted to confiscate, especially those in accounts abroad. There also were motions concerning support for Paul. Guardianship of him had been awarded to Cecilia at Rosario's wish.

Federal district judge Claude M. Hilton, who would preside over the trial, if there was one, decided on five hundred dollars a month, but it had to come from the account that Rick had set up for Cecilia in Bogotá. Lawyer Cummings argued that it was Cecilia's own money and not from Rick's ill-gotten gains. Hilton didn't buy it.

On March 30, Cecilia left for Bogotá with Paul. Shortly thereafter, the Colombian government granted him citizenship following a request from Rosario.

All Rick was demanding now was a deal for Rosario. But the best Cummings could obtain was a sentence of sixty-three to seventy-eight months for a guilty plea.

What about Pollard's wife? Rick complained. Did she get off so lightly just because he was giving secrets to Israel instead of Russia?

The irony was that if the internal security section

of the Justice Department—backed by the FBI—
hadn't won the day against the department's top leadership in having Rosario arrested, Rick wouldn't have
been ready to plead guilty to anything, much less
cooperate with the CIA. Rosario was the leverage.

In a confidential letter, dated April 22, Plato
Cacheris laid it all out for Rick:

> We have reached the stage where you must
> decide whether or not to enter a plea of guilty
> to espionage and conspiracy to commit tax
> evasion. Such a plea by you will result in a
> sentence of life imprisonment without parole.
>
> As Preston and I have repeatedly explained,
> you have every right to a trial by jury and
> the consequences of such a trial would not be
> detrimental to your case or sentence. While we
> cannot make any predictions or promises, you
> may fare better at a trial.
>
> If you forgo a trial, you would also specifi-
> cally abandon the following legal challenges:
>
> (1) the warrantless search of your office
> computer on June 25, 1993;
>
> (2) the legality of searches of your home,
> office, car, and hotel room [in Miami], pursuant
> to the Attorney General's executive order;
>
> (3) the legality of searches of your home,
> car, and computer under the Foreign Intelli-
> gence Surveillance Act;
>
> (4) the possibility of having your case sev-
> ered for trial from that of Rosario;
>
> (5) objections to the use of Rosario's con-
> fession against you in a joint trial;
>
> (6) the argument that the evidence against
> you is insufficient and deficient, and the corol-
> lary argument that, despite the massive per-
> sonal and electronic surveillance of you, the

government cannot establish that you passed one secret document or you met with one Russian agent;

(7) your appeal concerning the court's freezing of your assets, both foreign and domestic. . . .

At your express instructions, we have negotiated leniency for Rosario with the understanding that you will not receive any benefits on your sentence . . . [Rosario's] exact sentence may be influenced by your performance in debriefing sessions with government agents. . . .

We don't have to remind you that we have consistently recommended that you should litigate this case and not plead guilty. However, we are mindful of the fact that this is your case, and we cannot withhold our acquiescence from your decision to aid Rosario by pleading guilty.

There was one last-ditch plan to remove Rosario from the picture. Cacheris didn't think that the government was dying to prosecute Rosario separately. It had already granted that there was no proof that she had passed any secrets herself or operationally aided Rick in any meaningful way. If she first pleaded not guilty, and then he pleaded guilty, he could take the stand and testify that she was an innocent. The downside, as her lawyer told her, was that conceivably she could wind up with a much stiffer sentence. Rosario considered it and lost her nerve.

On April 28, Rick and Rosario both entered guilty pleas on espionage and tax evasion conspiracy charges. For the counts Rick pleaded to, he received the maximum sentence—life in prison without the possibility of parole.

Rosario would receive a minimum of sixty-three

months on lesser charges of espionage. Her actual sentence was to be delayed until August 26 and would be contingent on the degree of cooperation that Rick provided the CIA and the FBI. Both agreed not to appeal their sentences.

Rick gave up his CIA pension. Both forfeited all their assets, including foreign and domestic bank accounts, investment portfolios, the North Arlington house, all its furnishings, all personal jewelry and other objects of value, and the Jaguar and Honda. As a concession, the government agreed not to try to seize the property that Rick had acquired in Colombia.

Rick's sister, Nancy, was allowed to sell some two thousand volumes in his library to a McLean bookseller. One of them was a book of mine, *Manhunt*, which was about another pursuit and capture— that of an ex-CIA contract agent, Edwin P. Wilson, who, among other things, sold twenty tons of plastic C-4 explosive to the Libyan terrorist regime of Muammar el-Qaddafi. She sent the proceeds, unannounced, to Cecilia in Colombia for Paul.

At his sentencing, Rick accepted the court's offer to speak. His wife, he said in an eight-page statement, had "understood me to be cooperating with Russia, a country which she had heard extolled by Presidents Bush and Clinton as a friend and potential security partner."

He said, "I would like the court and the public to understand, in the context of this plea agreement, how it is that my beloved wife has agreed to spend many years in jail. She has been the object of a purposeful, vindictive campaign of villification by the government, designed to demoralize her, pressure me, and to destroy her reputation here and in her native country. The government has used the threat of a life sentence for her to obtain our agreement to this plea."

As for his own actions, he waxed philosophically about spying in general. "I had come to believe," he declared, "that the espionage business as carried out by the CIA and a few other American agencies was and is a self-serving sham, carried out by careerist bureaucrats who have managed to deceive several generations of American policymakers and the public about both the necessity and the value of their work."

If he had felt that strongly about this, Rick, of course, could have resigned from the agency and gone public with his critique. He did not, however, mention this option. Instead, as he put it, he decided to level the playing field. The truth was, he said, that "our counterintelligence efforts have had dramatic success since the mid-1950s. Despite decades of scare-mongering by bureaucrats who know better, American counterintelligence, the CIA, the FBI, and the military services, have effectively penetrated and manipulated the Soviet and Warsaw Pact intelligence services on a massive scale. . . . Frankly, these spy wars are a sideshow which have had no real impact on our significant security interests over the years."

Rick reserved two sentences of regret for persons in the "former Soviet Union and elsewhere" who might have suffered from his actions. "We made similar choices," he said, "and suffer similar consequences."

Unfortunately, the bullet-ridden Valery Martynov and the tortured Sergei Motorin, among others, were not available to compare their respective fates.

16

In her subsequent debriefings, Rosario, when questioned about finances, would snap, "Why do you keep asking me about money? Why do you keep bringing up money? Why do you say when did I know Rick had a lot of money? Why are you asking me this? It's not me that has a problem with money, it's you Americans who have the problem. In Bogotá, we never ask anybody how they got their money."

Agent Danielle Linden, who was brought in to do most of the interrogations of Rosario, remembered thinking, Well, if you asked somebody in Bogotá a question like that, the chances were that you'd be shot.

Rosario acknowledged that Rick had not immediately told her at the time they were married that investments involving "his Chicago friend, Robert" were the reason for Rick's sudden influx of cash. She said that in Mexico City, it had always been her impression that money was no concern for Rick. And then any financial straits he was in when she arrived in Washington were because of Rick's pending divorce. It was only in Rome, with the Swiss bank accounts now part of their lives, that "Robert" had been invoked.

She said that it was not true that she had an affair with the CIA case officer in Mexico City who recruited her and introduced her to Rick.

The officer, now out of the CIA, was living in California. Agent Dell Spry was sent to interview him.

"See my attorney," he told Spry.

When Spry did just that, the attorney said, "My client won't talk to you unless you grant him immunity."

"Immunity from what? How can we grant immunity unless we know what it's for?"

"I'm stating to you that my client won't talk to you without immunity. That's it."

"Well," said Spry, "we'll just subpoena his ass in front of a grand jury and fly him back and he'll have to testify."

"You do that," the attorney said, "and it'll be for nothing. You'd be wasting government money. He'll take the Fifth."

The FBI decided not to pursue Rosario's previous sex life. What difference did it make? By then, the bureau was convinced that she had not played a positive role in Rick's dealings with the Soviets. She'd just gone along with it. That was all that mattered.

For the same reason, the bureau did not press her on exactly when she had learned what Rick was doing and where the money really was coming from. She was consistently ruled "deceptive" on polygraphs when she named August 1992 as the time frame of her great discovery. She elaborated on the piece of paper she had found folded in an old wallet of Rick's that led her to question him. In addition to "our embassy," she said, there also was a typed reference to "the city in which your mother-in-law lives" that had frightened her. But neither she—nor Rick—could ever recall the exact message with any precision.

Rick was debriefed for approximately three hundred hours, principally, for the FBI, by Rudy Guerin.

He readily admitted to having supplied Moscow with the names of Martynov and Motorin, the London KGB *rezident* Gordievsky, the "spy dust" KGB officer in Moscow, the GRU officer stationed in Lisbon, the Bulgarian walk-in in Rome, and GRU general Dimitr Polyakov. "Yeah, I gave those guys up," he said.

Gradually, he recalled the others he had doomed. He also spoke of many additional compromises in operations, the details of which he sometimes could not specifically remember. He had passed on so much information, so many documents about so many operations, that he couldn't recall them all. However, there were more than thirty major compromises that he was able to pinpoint.

"I was, you know, sleepwalking then," he'd say. Or, "I was doing that one with blinders on. And after it was done, I washed it out. What the hell!"

He spoke of his frustration in setting up a meeting in 1985 with the Soviet diplomat Sergei Chuvakhin, which had started everything, and how, no matter what, on that fateful afternoon of April 16, he was determined to walk into the Soviet embassy.

He said that in his opinion, Vitaly Yurchenko was a genuine defector who had changed his mind largely because of the CIA's mishandling of him.

From FBI counterintelligence photographs, he identified his KGB handler "Vlad" as Vladimir Metchulayev and "Andrei" as Lieutenant Colonel Yuri Karetkin.

He insisted that he had worked alone for Moscow at Langley. He said he knew of no others like him, although, he added with a smirk, that didn't mean that there weren't any.

"Have you passed on identities that haven't been rolled up yet?" Guerin asked.

Rick said, "No."

He indulged in diatribes against the CIA—what a joke it really was. But he confessed that what had propelled him was greed. Money. Rosario.

He confessed, though, that he had gotten a "rush" out of what he was doing. He got almost orgasmic about it with Guerin. This was the reason he hadn't informed Moscow about his unexpected, second agency polygraph or his interview during the Playactor phase of the investigation. He had feared that Moscow might break off relations with him.

Oleg Gordievsky, CIA code name "Tickle," had escaped ultimate KGB retribution in a daring rescue out of Moscow engineered by the British Secret Service.

And despite Rick's best efforts, two others he'd betrayed had managed to evade the executioner's song.

One was Boris Yuzhin, the KGB lieutenant colonel stationed in San Francisco. Arrested in Moscow in 1986 after being named in Rick's "big dump," he protested that he had been blackmailed by the FBI over a relationship with an American girl but had provided erroneous information to the bureau. And he was able to demonstrate that he had rebuffed CIA recruitment once he was back safely in the Soviet Union. So instead of a firing squad, he got a harsh Gulag prison sentence, which one rarely survived. But in 1992, in a general political amnesty granted by Boris Yeltsin, he was released.

The other one was Sergei Fedorenko, the Soviet diplomat at the United Nations whom Rick had debriefed in New York and whom he had finally given up to "Vlad" in Rome. With his highly placed connections in the Soviet ruling elite, especially his ambassadorial father, Fedorenko was able to brazen it out, denying everything. And for once, the KGB was hesitant. The only evidence that the KGB had was Rick's word, and before anything more could be done, the Soviet empire began to crumble.

In 1992, Fedorenko was back in the United States, teaching at a college in Rhode Island. After Rick was sentenced, Rudy Guerin spent a day with Fedorenko in Washington and got a taste of his inbred élan. It was late when they finished talking. Guerin offered to put up Fedorenko in a hotel for the night at government expense. Fedorenko declined. He wanted to get back home to New England. Besides, he said with a jaunty air, if he had to stay over, he knew of a vacant house in North Arlington, Virginia.

In Bogotá, it was an article of faith among the cognoscenti that Rosario had been the victim of a cruel and manipulative *Yanqui*.

And in September, her sentencing was postponed when she requested a change in her legal representation, claiming that her court-appointed lawyer had advised her badly in her plea bargain. Her new attorney was a respected member of the Washington bar, John Hume. On instructions from Rosario, her mother had sold the ranch property in Colombia and used part of the proceeds to retain him.

Rosario could not appeal her sentence. But she could change her plea to not guilty. Actually, she was not going to do this. But the strategy involved here was to make the government think that it might happen, raising the presumably unwelcome specter of prosecuting her alone, with Rick, already serving life, as a witness on her behalf.

The thought was that the government would then

agree to at least a reduction of her sentence to, perhaps, two years, which, with time served, would have her released from prison even sooner. But it became evident that John Martin, the head of the Justice Department's internal security section, who had insisted on Rosario's original arrest complaint and warrant, was not going along with this.

Television and print reporters had been clamoring for in-depth interviews of Rosario. Hume decided on two of them he thought might sympathetically portray Rosario as a victim, swaying public perception of her and possibly—who knew?—the sentencing federal judge, Claude M. Hilton.

One was Diane Sawyer, the anchor on ABC's *Prime Time Live.* On the show, Rosario told Sawyer of Rick, "I despise him."

Sawyer asked, "Did you say to him, 'Are you crazy? Are you mad? You've got to stop.' "

"I did. I did. I told him, that was the one thing I insisted on, I told him, 'You have to stop, whatever it is, you have to stop. You have to stop' and he promised he would. . . ."

(Rosario conveniently forgot that when Rick returned with his last cache of cash from "Andrei" in Bogotá in November 1993, she did not say anything along the lines of hoping, finally, that it was over. Instead, her immediate interest concerned his next scheduled trip—for his next bundle of money.)

Rosario also changed another part of her story. In her statement to the FBI the day of her arrest, she said that Rick had told her Moscow wanted pictures of her and their son, but he had refused to turn them over. Her new version to Sawyer was that Rick had actually given the Russians photos of herself and Paul—*and* her mother—which caused her to live in constant trepidation.

Hume awarded a second interview to the Washington celebrity and writer Sally Quinn. Quinn's article, more than a full page in length, appeared in *The Washington Post*.

In it, Quinn likened Rosario's situation—her inability to report what Rick was doing ("Why did she put up with it?")—to that of a battered wife.

(After having listened to Rosario for the better part of eight months dominate the Ames household, verbally abuse Rick at every opportunity, continually castigate and humiliate him, and also scream at Paul, agents Julie Johnson and Mike Degnan burst out laughing when they read this.)

Quinn quoted Rosario about the deterioration of their marriage, especially in Rome. His impotence. "Rick started becoming indifferent, showing less and less interest in, let's say, the sexual part of our relationship, which was very hurtful to me."

Rosario, tears rolling down her face, told Quinn, "Oh, when I remember way back in 1982 when I met him . . . I did love him, and that's what hurts more. . . . Deep down I don't think he knew what it meant to love somebody. I don't think he really cared for anyone except Paul."

Quinn concluded: "She is certainly not perfect. She made some terrible choices. She has pleaded guilty to espionage. Is what she has done enough to sentence her to more than five years in prison, take away her freedom, confiscate everything she has ever owned, separate her from her family and from her only child? Judge Claude M. Hilton will make that decision Friday morning."

It was to no avail. On October 21, 1994, Hilton sentenced Rosario to the agreed-upon minimum sentence of sixty-three months.

There were fallouts from the Ames case.

A huge uproar in Congress erupted when it was

learned the CIA director, James Woolsey, had decided that no one would be dismissed or demoted at the agency in the aftermath of Rick's machinations. Instead, only letters of reprimand would be sent to eleven responsible top-level officers, including the deputy director of covert operations and the inspector general.

"Some have clamored for heads to roll in order that we could say that heads have rolled," Woolsey declared. "Sorry, that's not my way. And in my judgment, that's not the American way and it's not the CIA's way."

Woolsey was subsequently forced to resign, although the official version was that he had made the decision on his own.

In the wake of Plato Cacheris's threat to challenge the legality of the FBI's searches and seizures in Rick's home and office without the granting of a traditional search warrant required in criminal cases, Congress passed a new law giving the Foreign Intelligence Surveillance Court that specific power. At the time Cacheris brought up the issue, the Justice Department treated it dismissively. Then, Rick's guilty plea made it moot.

"Certainly, [Cacheris] had raised those issues and threatened to litigate," explained Deputy Attorney General Jamie Gorelick. "And anytime you don't have a Supreme Court case on point, there's always a risk. We thought we would prevail, but . . . this, I think, cements it."

Perhaps most significant of all, although largely ignored by the media, was a dramatic change in the leadership of CIA counterespionage. Despite an all-out effort by the agency to prevent his appointment, it would be run—*at Langley*—by an FBI agent, Edward J. Curran Jr., chosen by Louis Freeh on the recommendation of Bear Bryant.

Rick Ames, meanwhile, was besieged with requests by newspapers, magazines, television networks, and radio for interviews.

He had already been interviewed in *The New York Times,* the *Los Angeles Times,* and *The Washington Post* before he made his first televised appearance. At his choice, it was on CNN worldwide cable. It was the one network that he knew would be watched in Moscow. He had requested that it be carried live, but this was turned down. In the back of everyone's mind, including Rick's, was the fact that the Russians still owed him a lot of money, at least a million dollars, that could be paid to Rosario on her return to Bogotá.

He later appeared on National Public Radio, even on the BBC. More print interviews followed. And although he quickly admitted to being a traitor, he turned the interviews into rather high-flown discourses on the efficacy of the spy trade in general, what it all meant in the long run.

He loved it all, Rudy Guerin reminisced, being a celebrity. But everybody was missing the point.

Rick Ames was far more than a traitor. There were traitors like John Walker and Jonathan Pollard. All they did, though, was pass paper. "Rick killed people, at least twelve of them that we know of," Rudy Guerin said. "He was a bloody murderer."

And one without remorse.

In one of the last sessions Guerin had with Ames, he asked, "Rick, if you had to do it all over again, what would you choose? The CIA or the KGB?"

Without a second's hesitation, Rick Ames said, "The KGB."

CPSIA information can be obtained at www.ICGtesting.com
Printed in the USA
LVOW11s0301270315

432257LV00001B/11/P